Holiday Writes

Edited by Betty Dobson

InkSpotter Publishing

Holiday Writes

PUBLISHED BY INKSPOTTER PUBLISHING
163 Main Avenue, Halifax, Nova Scotia, Canada B3M 1B3
http://inkspotter.com/

Printed and bound in the United States of America by CreateSpace

Library and Archives Canada Cataloguing in Publication

Holiday writes : celebrations throughout the year & around the world / edited by Betty Dobson.

Includes index.
ISBN 978-0-9739896-0-1

1. Holidays—Literary collections. 2. Christmas—Literary collections.
I. Dobson, Betty, 1962-

PN6071 H7H64 2007   808.8'0334   C2007-903147-1

Dedicated to the child in all of us

Table of Contents

FROM THE EDITOR...V

NEW YEAR 1

Musing Over a New Calendar..3
Unresolved...4
Black Eyed Peas and Ham Hocks..5
New Year...6

EASTER 7

How Easter Really Began 9
Easter 16

GETAWAYS 17

Cut-Price Paradise 19
A Bunch of Rocks: The Environmental Gutting of Malta..........................21
Days of the Dead 25

IN MEMORIAM 29

Their Names Liveth Forevermore...31
Flags 33

THANKSGIVING..35

Tracing Back Thanksgiving Tradition...37
The First Thanksgiving 39
Turkey Therapy 41
Excess and Dad's Exes..42
The Day After Thanksgiving Holiday..43

CHRISTMAS 47

Always Home 49

So This is Christmas..50
Holiday Giving 52
A Time-Honoured Tradition...53
December..56
Dear Santa..57
Australian Christmas Holiday...59
Christmas Grows on Trees..61
Christmas Without You 63
Winter Solstice 66
Happy Holidays You Bah-Hum-Buggin' Vamps..................................67
Oy! It's Christmas Again!..68
Deck the Halls… 69
Thirteen Plates 71
The Christmas Dragon 73
Christmas trees enthralled in light 76
A Dash of Cinnamon, a Pinch of the Past, a Smidgen of the Future........77
Our Little Floozy 79
Christmas Alight 81
Christmas in Miramichi 84
Luminarias 85
Hurrah the Saturnalia! 86
Reflections from Shadow*...87
Boxing Day at the North Pole 90
Peace On Earth…and In Your Home, Too 91
Joyful Noise..93

HANUKAH..95

Hanukah Harry..97
Miracle 99

AUTHOR BIOS... 101

AUTHOR INDEX 109

From the Editor

Holiday Writes started on a small scale in 2005 when I asked my newsletter readers for holiday-themed submissions for the December issues of *InkSpotter News* and *Heritage Writer*. I received far more than I could possibly use but quickly saw the potential to expand the theme into a bigger venue.

The stories and poems in this anthology run the full gamut from cynical to sentimental, with a fair amount of humour tossed in. And, as the subtitle suggests, we cover a lot more than Christmas. *Holiday Writes* may be enjoyed, in whole or in part, throughout the year.

The term "holiday" is interpreted somewhat loosely here. While most events are "national" holidays, three essays deal with vacations (otherwise known as holidays in some parts of the world).

We've got writers from the United States and Canada, the United Kingdom and Australia, India and Germany. Some are established authors. Others are still looking for their big breakthroughs. All are vital parts of this anthology.

Betty Dobson
Editor/Publisher

New Year

Musing Over a New Calendar

Carolyn Howard-Johnson

Pencil essentials from last year's
memos, errant e-mail addresses, birth
days from last year to next.
Once a task of anticipation, now
tired, a roll of lives lost.
No need to keep Noni's
Libra date, or Hazel's
amethyst entry. I hear myself
whimper. When we moved
to Phoenix a woman of pioneer stock
said that was where her friends
went to flake off. She is gone
a long time ago, peeling
layers like a rich croissant
I prefer to think. Reality
is not an option. Grandma Ruthie
lamented growing old means
watching friends die. Those words
only months before she spade
the bitter earth to scatter
Utah's loam on father's
grave, he barely 64, too young
to see grandchildren
marry, I now the same age as he.
So much to write, so much
to see. India's colours, Tibet's heights,
Tierra del Fuego's stars all want
me. But Mother's alone, rejects
all but her home. Fiercely. I turn
the planner's page,
wait for another December
to take its bite from her life.
Or mine.

Unresolved

Betty Dobson

I made no resolutions,
Spoke no promises aloud,
Yet held expectations
In quiet reserve.

So much for not smoking
And for watching my weight.
I missed every birthday
And lost a friend.

Still stuck in a day job
That pays too many bills
And can't exorcise the harsh
Critic inside.

Black Eyed Peas and Ham Hocks

Thelly Reahm

How could anything as distasteful to me as black-eyed peas and ham hocks, buttermilk and cornbread bring good luck? I wondered as I stirred the pot of beans simmering on the stovetop. Little bits of ham were flavouring the distasteful beans as they cooked, but not even the wonderful flavour of ham could disguise the weird taste of those peas. And why did they call them peas? They had no resemblance to peas at all. However, that did give me pause, because I don't like peas either. It's not the peas actually; it's that mealy feel of them on my tongue. I love pea soup, hate peas! Hate lima beans for the same reason, but love lima bean soup!

"Why do you cook black-eyed peas every year if you don't like them?" Richie asked.

"A New Year's Day tradition is a New Year's Day tradition! My Grandma said if you eat black-eyed peas on New Year's Day it brings good luck." I smiled.

"Well, that doesn't make sense." He turned to leave the room. He probably needed more space between the smell of the bean pot and his sensitive nose.

"No more than your daughter, Linda, fixing rutabagas for Thanksgiving (and nobody eats them). That's a Benett tradition. Where did the Reahm tradition of 'sick eggs' come from?"

"Well, that's different! Sick eggs taste good!"

It seems we only approve of the baggage that we bring along to the table! On the other hand, truly obedient people, even though they don't like the taste of something, keep the tradition alive! I was always a compliant child!

Drat those black-eyed peas!

New Year

Carolyn Howard-Johnson

Resolutions are resolute,
                    irons around my pen.
Goals shackle

                    the sun that colours
                    cotton candy clouds.
                    They must wait for
                    noon's plans. They

              WEIGH the wind,
              REGIMENT the light,
              REGULATE the rhyme
              TIE me to a plan.

Resolution cannot write,
                    pulse my heart,
                    rouse my loins
                    or call the quail at early dawn.

Resolute defies thought
              INHIBITS meter's ebb and flow,
              SILENCES song,
              QUASHES milkweed's seeds in flight

Every year these twins stand before me. Chill winds
              disperse January's promise.
              Unfettered inspiration scattered
              irretrievable in the name of tradition.

Easter

How Easter Really Began
E.D. Easley

The roots of Easter, as a religious event, go back a couple thousand years. It means different things to different people, depending how you pay homage to your supreme being.

Some folks say what happened on Easter caused us to evolve spiritually on a scale Darwin would be proud of.

But in Capitalist America, it's not very noble. It's just another example of how Professional Liars, bean counters, and bureaucrats can screw up a perfectly beautiful thing.

In Capitalist America, there's an ugly aspect of the nondenominational Easter celebration that's been covered up by the government. The few of those who know the real story behind America's Capitalist Easter believe we made a horrible mistake.

We just collect our eggs, gather together, eat a fine dinner, and praise whatever lord we praise for the miracle we praise Him for.

That, by the way, isn't cynical. Different people believe in different things about Easter. Don't shoot the messenger; just have a nice day, okay?

So how did America's Capitalist Easter start? To tell the real story, you have to cut through the crap...

It promised to be one of those fine spring mornings you only get in Hanford, Washington. The sun barely touched the horizon with just a hint of shimmering green haze. If you breathed deep, there was the slightest whiff of ozone in the air.

Grandpa Jones sat on the porch. His home was straight out of a Norman Rockwell painting—down to the white picket fence. It was built around the turn of the nineteenth century and was near listing on the National Register.

It had a wide front porch, and he was sitting in his old rocking chair, just waiting for the sun to come up. He had a bowl full of cherry tobacco burning lazily in his seasoned pipe. The old, white-haired man felt right at home here, where he was born and had grown up. He'd met and married his high school sweetheart here, and they went to the town school before it burned down. Their kids had grown up here. They worked in town.

And now there was little Billy...

This place had been a cattle ranch once. The cows had all died. These days not a whole lot other than scrub brush grew in these parts.

His home was one of the few places left standing from the old days. Hanford sprang up largely during the Second World War. They built The First Bombs here. The ones that brought Japan to its knees. Einstein hung out at the soda shop in town sometimes. Once he bought Grandpa Jones an ice cream soda.

But then, Grandpa Jones had just been a kid at the time. He was an old man now...

He was still rocking when little Billy came out on the porch. Billy was a blonde, blue-eyed boy. At five, he was too smart for his own good. It was Easter morning, and this was probably the last year he'd believe in an Easter Bunny.

Five was a long time to believe, but this was Hanford. Folks around here played by a different set of rules than a lot of folks.

He came right up to his grandpa, crawled up into the old man's lap, and began to rock.

"Tell me again, Grandpa," he pleaded, "how did Easter start?"

Jones sighed and stroked his white beard. He knew there was no use telling the kids in Hanford The Big Lie forever. Around here, sooner or later they learned the truth.

Kids who grew up in the Nuclear Triangle—the Tri Cities everyone called them—in south central Washington state—eventually learned they lived in a nuclear dump. Folks joked about the water in the area, though those jokes really weren't funny to anyone with the smarts to really test it.

The air was just as bad. While Nagasaki and Hiroshima were ground zero for the only nuclear bombs man has ever detonated, those bombs had to be made somewhere. And when they were made, being the first of their kind, there were some—well—mistakes with the raw material.

Not that the mistakes blew up or anything, but the by products had to be put somewhere. No, nuclear accidents aren't much to write home about if you live next door to them. Not at first anyway.

As disasters go, nuclear accidents tend to be, well, quiet.

As time went on America started to build nuclear plants to generate power. They promised us this would be more clean and efficient than burning coal.

Then there were the guys with pointy heads and stars on their shoulders. They convinced presidents and congresses that more nuclear weapons would be a great way to keep communists from taking over the world.

True, the communists didn't take over the world—but there was a problem with the clean power thing and nasty weapons.

Making nukes generated waste. Really bad waste that glowed in the dark for something like a billion years. Mankind would probably come and go—heck, a whole new race of dinosaurs may be born and become extinct—but the nuclear waste would still be out there…as toxic as ever.

So The Folks Who Make The Rules in America, the government bureaucrats, got together on this one. It was a problem—one of those Really Big Ones they figured they'd better get right if they wanted to act responsibly.

But then, in the true calling of great American bureaucrats everywhere, they acted in character. They passed the buck. And this time they passed it on in historic proportions.

They realized one of the true bureaucratic truths of the Nuclear Mess. Nuclear waste was a very long-term problem, and on the universal scale of things the period of time they'd be around was pretty damn short.

So by the time the whole thing really hit the fan, they'd be long gone.

The first problem America faced was how to deal with the exhausted nuke fuel rods and other really nasty poisonous by products. Sure, they were considered too pumped out to heat Chicago or Boston, but they were still pretty radioactive and poisonous, so well, we had to put them somewhere.

Hanford was a great spot. It was out in the desert anyway. We'd already thrown out a bunch of stuff that glowed in the dark out in that desert, so well, America's really toxic trash headed out West.

Why not use that big old stretch of scrub brush as America's toxic toilet? The bureaucrats reasoned it was pretty close to where a lot of the mess was made.

And any real estate agent will tell you; it's all about location, location, location!

One of the problems with all government projects is the help. The U.S. government is probably the world's largest employer, and the lousiest outfit to work for.

In this case, it started right from the beginning.

Somebody had to do things like move the uranium around and keep things neat and clean.

There was a war going on when America was building The Bomb, and folks handling the project had a huge natural non-union resource: Army enlisted men. Talk about an ideal bunch of employees…you could tell them to do anything and they couldn't quit. Hell, you could put them in jail for talking back to you.

You could go so far as to tell them to die for you. Indeed, that's what a whole lot of them were doing in World War II.

So imagine how relieved some of those Army guys were when they found themselves assigned to a post in central Washington State.

Sweet duty, huh? There wasn't a whole lot in the desert shooting back at them except an occasional farmer if they got too friendly with their daughters. Granted there were a few snakes out in the desert, but they came to find out rattlesnake tasted kind of like chicken.

Even so, it beat dodging bullets or artillery.

Back in the Forties, scientists knew nuclear material was dangerous, but they had no idea how dangerous it was. They often shipped it from coast to coast by train and truck.

Well, in Hanford a lot of that stuff had to travel to the bomb-making plant on dirt roads by truck at first. More than once the drivers did things like stop to have a smoke, tend to bodily functions, hit large animals, or run over stray Indians. Sometimes they fell asleep at the wheel.

More than once their trucks overturned.

When these things happened, the scientists at the Manhattan project freaked out. They weren't worried as much about the project's security as they were about meeting the deadline the feds had imposed on them. America's Jap and Kraut killers wanted themselves a means of mass destruction—and they wanted it now!

So under the guise of patriotism, they pushed production of the worst damn thing that had ever fallen out of the sky. Something so horrible it would only take two to end a global wrestlemania.

Later, asked why he used two nukes, Harry Truman responded, "I only had two."

But to the scientists rushing to meet that deadline, it was mostly a contract—and you don't go on screwing up federal contracts if you want to keep getting big, fat government grants.

And a scientist who didn't get grants was a dork who wasn't going to keep beans on the table. All the dorks at Hanford knew their work meant guaranteed academic fame and fortune—and fat grants for life.

The fact is they only hand out so many Nobel prizes, and these bright boys figured they had a shot at a few—if they played their cards right.

Early in the nuke game, as was typical for the government, the right hand wasn't communicating with the left hand. Some of the world's finest dorks gravitated to Hanford—but the military support was, well, lacking.

In one month, for example, three truckloads of nuclear material overturned on the way to Hanford. The scientists were livid. Some of the fuel was lost in the scrub brush; a chunk of it was unaccounted for. And unless it was found, they'd miss their deadline.

Missing a deadline was a big deal to dorks. The guys with the stars on their shoulders and the pointy heads wanted their bombs now.

Scientists are usually really good at dealing with theories and numbers. Most of them can stand in front of blackboards and do complex calculations all day. But a whole lot of them don't deal well with people. They don't like confrontations, and they don't want to screw with the business of personnel management.

So they slough that stuff off to some schmuck.

The schmuck early on at Hanford was a lieutenant colonel charged with the business of securing the place. Technically it was considered a military reservation, and he was a Provost Marshal by trade. He had a dozen or so guys with guns under him who really didn't want to shoot anything.

So the head scientist, well, the dork the other guys shoved out the door, told the top cop they needed more nuke stuff. The top cop shrugged and explained how he only had enough peons to lock down the joint surrounded by barbed wire.

And it was tough shit they'd lost some Really Nasty Crap in the desert. They should order some more.

That's just how it was done in the government. Especially in wartime.

In the 1940s folks didn't just wave their hands and get processed nuclear material. In fact, making the stuff that made The Big Bang was what they were doing out at Hanford. The Top Cop's attitude represented a big problem.

The head scientist tried to get more material. He called folks in D.C. At first they laughed at him. They thought he was joking. There was some funny joke still floating around D.C. about what the dorks did with those rods. It's best not told around small children or in mixed company.

After the guys in Washington stopped laughing, they asked the dork how hard could it be to find pounds of stuff that glowed in the dark along the only road for miles in a desert? They asked him what his degree was in and hung up on him.

The head scientist didn't know how to take a joke. They hadn't taught that course in graduate school.

He stopped by the lieutenant colonel's office and repeated the whole conversation to him. The colonel, an activated reserve officer, still had some common sense left in him.

And he came up with a plan.

He looked into the installation's reserve fund—a kind of emergency piggy bank—and found a huge chunk of change. He used it as the first of many slush funds Hanford would see over the years.

He'd already considered the staff at Hanford. It was a sorry collection of specialists who couldn't bribe their way out of a paper bag if it had ten holes in it. He considered his military contingent, but there weren't enough of those to do anything other than fill up a small bar. There were the union guys, who wouldn't do anything outside their contracts. Then there were the scientists...again, he realized he didn't have any pool of labour to work with.

Then he thought about the local folks. He just wanted them to spend one morning before the sun came up looking for pellets that glowed in the dark. All they had to do was walk along the road and pick them up.

The colonel figured he'd pay a tidy sum for every pellet they brought in. Under this plan everybody won. The locals made a few bucks, the scientists got their pellets back, and the jerks in D.C. left him alone.

So he wadded up some hundred-dollar bills, threw them all over the place, and did it.

As luck would have it, the first collection of really nasty crap happened on Easter Sunday, 1940. It rapidly became something of a social event for the folks in Hanford, and by 1950 had spread nationally to the event we observe today.

In Hanford they're still collecting those "special eggs". Bunches of them are still lying around out in the desert. Folks who run the nuclear dump lose them all the time.

And yes, you can still take them right up to the gate of the government reservation. They'll run a Geiger counter over them and can tell the difference between them and all the rest of the local background radiation.

There's an awful lot of background radiation in that neighbourhood to start with.

They'll give you money for as many special eggs you find. And it doesn't have to be just on Easter these days. They pay off all year round. Guys in thick, white suits come out to the gate to collect your eggs and put them on special boxes.

For some reason, they never hand a check to you. They always pass it though a thick, glass window in a concrete box.

But today it was just one more Easter in the Tri Cities.

Grandpa looked out as the sun barely peeked over the horizon. He smiled at his grandson. "I'll tell you the story about the Easter Bunny again after you come back in," he told the boy. "But it's time for you to go out and look for eggs."

Little Billy smiled, nodded, and slid off his Grandpa's lap. He blinked that one big blue eye in the middle of his face.

"Remember, Billy," Grandpa smiled. "Only the ones that glow. We'll have a big breakfast later!"

"Yippee!" Billy cheered as he picked up his basket and tried not to let his flippers drag as he headed out into the desert.

Easter

Laurie Corzett

Gentle rosy raindrops of a mellow morning,
Children make the day—it's spring.
I thought of God in Church this morning,
nailed to His cross in long ago Jerusalem,
arising to springtime, the earth's reawakening.
It's a time for children and games of childhood,
a time for playing with love,
secret smiles and daisy chains.
It's a time for the simple and natural
A time for anointing the soul in peace
after the ravages of winter.
A time for gentle things
like newborn kittens
and flower buds after the rain.
I am slowly relearning the healing strength of love,
Slowly relearning the simple pleasures of humanity.
Life is sweet, poignant,
a drifting melody.

Getaways

Cut-Price Paradise

Mary Cook

"All the fun of the pie," proclaims the billboard. It once read: "All the fun of the pier" but the last letter dropped off long ago. British seaside resorts that saw their heyday between the reign of Queen Victoria and the 1950s retain a certain faded charm today. In fact it's that faint air of decay that gives them their enduring appeal.

Enterprising local authorities may hope to boost their holiday trade with major refurbishment schemes. But these are merely cosmetic surgery for old ladies—a superficial improvement while the endearing character remains the same. Their life experience is their strongest asset, when it's worn like a rakish hat with "kiss me quick" around the band.

Just the words "a day at the seaside" will ignite a spark of excitement in a child's eyes and bring the glow of nostalgia to those of any adult.

The British are an island race with the inbred urge to spend as much time as possible by, on or in their surrounding sea. Since the eleventh century when King Cnut somewhat apocryphally tried to tame it by holding back the tide, the Brits have loved to be beside the sea.

But it was during the days of Queen Victoria that the seaside holiday became the great British institution it remains today. Alfred Lord Tennyson, the Poet Laureate so beloved of Queen Victoria, spent boyhood holidays at Mablethorpe, the small seaside town that's still popular as a resort.

Bathing machines, those small huts on wheels in which people could change modestly into their bathing dress were introduced in the eighteenth century. But their popularity rose in the early nineteenth century, reaching their peak in Victorian times when sea bathing was prized for its supposed health-giving properties. Indeed, Queen Victoria had her own machine on the Isle of Wight.

Some resorts boasted a bathing woman whose duties included immersing bathers. Amazingly, they paid her to carry out this assault on their person in the interests of "health".

Bathing machines are a thing of the past. But you can still see plenty of bathing huts, their static successors, lighting up shorelines with their bright, albeit flaking, paint.

Place names trip off the tongue for the seaside enthusiast: Blackpool, Brighton, Mablethorpe, Margate, Scarborough, Skegness.

When you walk down the main street in most British seaside towns, don't forget to look up. The shop facades may be modern, but above them you'll see the rest of the building that has been left unaltered—elderly and gracious.

If you ask anyone what makes a seaside holiday you'll get a variety of answers:

Miles of sandy beaches where children can build sandcastles, a pier with slot machines, donkey-rides, candyfloss. It doesn't matter that the clock has stopped at a half past 1957.

Skegness, on the East Coast of England, dubbed the "Funcoast" by tourism chiefs, is one well-known resort that manages to combine all these favourites so that generations of visitors return year after year. It made it all the more surprising when, some years ago, a man stepped off a tourist bus and asked passers-by: "Excuse me—is there a sea here?"

"Skegness is so bracing!" said Skegness' Jolly Fisherman on a famous poster commissioned by The Great Northern Railway Company in 1908. And that's putting it mildly. The wind whips in off the North Sea blowing sand into sandwiches, eyes, clothes and hair—magical.

Donkeys have been given a raw deal over the years. But nowadays welfare schemes with regular health checks ensure they're well cared for. Skegness donkeys have been named the best in the country, with Bruno being nominated best donkey for his "professionalism".

Seaside holidays have long been seen as consolation prizes for the less affluent while better off members of society take holidays abroad, staying in hotels. For the seaside visitor, accommodation tends to be in a budget-style guest house or a hired caravan—a modest structure with basic amenities. Its main feature is that you can hear the rain on the roof above everything else.

Even today, the pull of the sea is irresistible, with people making their way to the coast at the first sign of a sunny weekend, travelling by whatever means they have at their disposal: car, train, coach, or hitch-hiking.

Ask any Englishman to recount his favourite holiday memory. It won't be the skiing holiday he took with the guys when they were all young and free; nor will it be his honeymoon, taken at bank-breaking expense in the Seychelles. The memory that will reduce him to misty-eyed nostalgia is of the week he spent with his family in a seaside caravan when he was just nine years old. It was cold; it was raining; and they enjoyed "all the fun of the pie". For that was the best holiday—ever!

A Bunch of Rocks: The Environmental Gutting of Malta

Betty Dobson

As you look down from the hillside onto the apparent perfection of Malta's Blue Lagoon, you struggle to imagine it in any other condition. Land embraces lagoon like a protective parent. Water shines like a molten blending of sapphires and emeralds. The perpetually cloudless sky appears hazy against such brilliance. Craggy islets guard the entrance like dorsal spines on some mythic leviathan. But you walk the Malta of the modern world, a Mediterranean archipelago where prehistoric temples, safely preserved within the womb of nature for millennia, are being eroded in less than a hundred years by pollution, vandalism, and the very air we exhale.

Who cares about a bunch of rocks? The majority of Maltese seem to care very little. Hunters consider the temples an obstruction and use the fragile stones for target practice. Lovers seek to immortalize their union by painting or scraping their initials onto the ancient surfaces. Even you, who consider the temples sacred, damage these walls with your presence. Each breath you expel adds to the gradual erosion of the stones. Still, you can't help but applaud the slow-moving wisdom of the government. They may close all the temples tomorrow, but you're seeing them today.

Then you realize that the damage extends far beyond the confines of the temples. Remnants of the human presence—chip bags, cigarette packages, and condom wrappers—litter roadsides and line the low stone walls of the countryside. A shiny black snake, barely a centimetre across, slides along the base of one of those walls. The fledgling leviathan sidles around an immovable juice bottle, then darts back to the wall, back to its meagre shelter from the noon sun. Legend holds that St. Paul robbed the island's snakes of their venom. Nature retaliated by placing the venom in the tongues of women. Even miracles lack surety. Most changes, even for the good, come with a price.

Malta's history is a study in change. In the centuries before becoming an independent republic in 1974, Malta played host to a series of conquerors and protectors. The archipelago's beginnings vanished in the fog of pre-history, but hints remain as to the nature of life among the ancients. Temple builders, they dedicated their lives to the fertile earth. By their own reckoning, both they and the temples came from the earth and returned to it in death. One might claim that Ggantija—one of the few surviving temples—is older than God. It certainly predates the pyramids at Giza by roughly a thousand years, making it the oldest freestanding structure yet unearthed.

Walking within the walls of Ggantija—or any of the temples— becomes a tactile experience. Touch the stones. Warmed by the sun, they seem alive with energy. Let your fingers play over the weathered texture, the spiral designs tracing the renewing cycle of life. Imagine them smooth with newness and the ceiling rebuilt. Let yourself slide into the role of priestess. Bless the children born of woman's fertility. Bless the harvest born of the Earth Mother's fertility. The serpents need not hide. They spin in circles, chasing their tails. More than mere aspect, they embody the design itself. Life starts and ends, and starts again.

Step back farther and see the ancient Mediterranean world, a vast, verdant continent—no Maltese archipelago, no Sicilian island, no Italian peninsula. Then the ocean rose, fracturing the land and exposing Malta like an unwanted child.

In modern times, garbage cuts a jagged path into the sea. Some items float on the surface, giving a hint of the damage that rests below. Even the Blue Lagoon, a favourite retreat among tourists and locals alike, bears the scars of abuse. You can't see them at first. The illusion of perfection holds too great a power.

Look over the rail of the tour boat. First you notice the clarity of the water, then the way the white sand bottom seems to reach up to the sun. Slim black fish, no more than three inches long, swim by in oblong schools like passing storm clouds. You take a few pictures to capture the images for others to see. Then you simply stare, letting the images develop in your memory.

A flurry of motion attracts your attention. The fish congeal into a pulsing mass, as if forming one creature. A flash of red and brown marks the centre. The predators have found their prey: a discarded candy bar wrapper. Each quivering attack sends the slick paper spinning. Only when they've picked the last of the brown meat from the white interior does their frenzy end. A lone fish breaks formation and approaches a new offering bobbing a few feet away. Like a tentative lover, it touches its lips to the morsel. Has it tasted nicotine before? One would think so, given its hasty retreat. No other fish repeats the experiment.

Malta, like so many modern cultures, feeds upon itself to prolong its existence. Honey-yellow limestone forms the core of the archipelago. When first quarried, the stone succumbs easily to the workers' tools. Exposure hardens the stone until it's as durable as concrete. Once used in the construction of temples, the stone now serves for everything from bridges to bus stops.

Meanwhile, the quarries seem to scream their pain and rage skyward. They're meant for conversion to farmland, but truckloads of landfill and topsoil can't keep pace with excavations. As the tour bus passes yet another crater, your guide smiles and assures you that there is enough limestone for at least two hundred more years of quarrying. The implication seems clear. Any event that will not occur during one's lifetime warrants minimal concern.

You can't help feeling grateful for your chance to experience a few of Malta's natural and constructed wonders. Reborn temples stake a sacred claim on the land and on your imagination. But upon each memory of grandeur, a corresponding sense of loss intrudes. The images stay with you: waste-devouring fish, polluted lagoons, eroding temples, and disembowelled earth. How much longer, you wonder, before Malta collapses in upon itself and litters the Mediterranean with its remains?

The future teeters on the present. If you could travel forward in time, what might you see? Perhaps nothing more than a single black snake, coiled within the arc of a floating juice bottle.

Days of the Dead

George Burden

We advanced quietly through the darkness-shrouded old ruins. Flickering candles drew us towards the nine-hundred-year-old Mayan pyramid of the Ruinas del Rey on this solemn night of October 31st. The people of the remote jungle village had traveled three hours to reach this sacred spot, the first time in over thirty years they had been permitted to do so.

Thirteen in number, we watched quietly as villagers lit candles and prepared sacred dishes of mole, pibe, tamale, and a drink of honey-sweetened raw chocolate. Perhaps the size of our group was coincidence, but the Maya consider thirteen to be a lucky number. It is the number of benign gods in their pantheon, sadly outnumbered by the nineteen evil deities, against which they struggle bravely to protect mankind.

The "Day of the Dead" should perhaps be more appropriately called the "Days of the Dead"; for from October 31st to November 2nd, all across Mexico, deceased loved ones are memorialized during this time. In urban areas the custom is treated much like our own Halloween, but in rural Mexico it is still an intensely religious holiday with roots going back into the mists of pre-Columbian times. Though now ostensibly Christianized, it is really an ancient Mayan rite that was moved to All Souls' and All Saints' Days. The celebrations remain a mélange of traditional and Christian religions.

The festival can be quite joyous. Indeed it is not unusual to welcome departed souls with graveside picnics complete with fireworks, mariachi bands, and flowers. It is also considered good luck to receive a sugar skull on which is inscribed your name. Carved skulls and skeletons reflect a pre-Columbian fascination with the calcified portions of human remains, evidence of which can be seen in ruins like Chichen Itza. Tonight however is especially dedicated to the souls of little children, the angelitos or little angels. Worshippers carry votive candles in paper containers (papel picado) many praying silently. The pungent aroma of incense rises and drifts among the columns of deserted temples, once packed with these villagers' ancestors. One of our group tells me she lost a small child years ago. A meteorite streaks reddishly across the sky behind the altar, a booth of palm fronds that looks surprisingly like the crèche for a nativity scene. My friend interprets this as a hello from her departed daughter.

Villagers consume the food for the offering and pass it around to guests. It is all prepared on site. I try some food and afterwards down a draught of honeyed chocolate, long a sacred drink before the Hispanic conquest. The shared sustenance seems to cement a bond between the simple villagers and onlookers. The ceremony ends, and we trudge back through the ruins.

November 1st, All Saints' Day. We cross the bay to the Isla de Mujeres or Island of Women. In ancient times this was the eastern-most outpost of the Maya, sacred because it was the first of their territory to receive the rays of the rising sun. The island is sacred to Ixchul, the goddess of the moon and of fertility. The remnants of her temple are found on the southern tip of the island. When Cortes, the conqueror of Mexico, first reached this island, he discovered a cache of female fertility figures here, hence the name. He smashed them all, as evidence of idolatry. The isle still remains a popular place of pilgrimage for those seeking fertility, both for locals and New-Agers from farther north. (I noticed one couple in a hammock who seemed to be testing the theory.)

For those less interested in getting pregnant there is a walking trail along the coral encrusted coast offering vistas of turquoise waters, sea birds, and the island of Cancun in the distance. There are some small coral caves where guests can seek tranquility or visitors can climb up to the statuary garden with its colourful and sometimes jarring works prefacing the approach to Ixchul's temple itself. Along the way, we passed through a charming and colourful reproduction of a Caribbean village, which also housed a small museum to the pirate Moncada. He made a fortune in the slave trade then, as legend fittingly has it, fell into an unrequited love affair with a native woman and died of a broken heart. The remains of the estate and garden he built, a vain attempt to lure his beloved into his arms, can still be seen farther north on the island.

For the more adventurous, an impressive network of zip lines offers rapid descents from the hills overlooking the beach at Garrafon Park. If you try it, use the brake sparingly or you'll find yourself dangling helplessly, fifteen meters above the water, waiting for one of the guides to come retrieve you. The hammock garden here offers relaxation and decadent views, but the much-touted snorkelling on the reef is a disappointment with rough murky waters and mostly dead coral. Our guides told us that efforts are being made to revitalize it.

November 2nd, All Souls' Day, dawned with our party journeying to Xcaret. Another ancient Mayan site, up the coast from Cozumel, it boasts some interesting ruins and a themed eco-park. It is a child-friendly place that features visits to a quite convincing reproduction of an ancient Mayan village. Here, locals of Mayan heritage make and sell crafts including gorgeous hand-woven blankets, colourful pottery, and figurines depicting Mayan deities and monarchs.

A unique option is to don a life vest and float through a seven-hundred-meter long underground river. I tried this and soon gained some understanding of how the damned souls in Dante's Inferno felt, floating along the River Styx. I didn't see any alluxians though (a leprechaun-like creature said to inhabit underground rivers in Mayan mythology). Another river system offers a float through deep, narrow gorges past the Mayan village on the banks high above.

Xcaret offers some more conventional experiences including a dolphin encounter for all ages. While this may be controversial to some, I can only conclude that the dolphins here are happy since they've been breeding like rabbits. The parks' two rare jaguars—the male jet-black, the female dappled—have a large island to themselves.

As a special treat, today's festivities include the grand opening of a new cemetery. The seven-tiered conical structure features 365 graves, each unique, representing the days of the year. Even today, Mayan structures mirror the pyramids of their forefathers with time-based architectural representations. To date there are no bodies interred here, though I understand people are dying to get in (at least judging from the line-ups to see the new burial ground). As well, I was gratified to see that large numbers of locals visit the park, a welcome respite from tourist attractions elsewhere in the Caribbean.

After the opening ceremonies, the park threw a grand fiesta with local cuisine and music. I decided to explore some out-of-the-way corners of the park a bit further and somehow found myself in an underground labyrinth of caves. Natural light came down through occasional holes in the limestone crust, but this was gradually fading as twilight approached. I became separated from my group and totally lost. Despite tantalizing strains of music, I was unable to find my way out and had dark visions of spending the rest of my days in some Mayan underworld. Finally, in desperation, I climbed up through a sinkhole, headed for the music, and stumbled onto a path just as the rest of the group passed by. The Mayan god of the foolish must have been smiling on me.

Rejoining the group, I learned that next on the agenda was a show, re-enacting pre-Hispanic Mayan rituals, the arrival of the conquistadors (on horseback no less), and various more modern musical fare. While owing at least a tithe to Vegas, the costumes and music were topnotch.

My final day was marked by packing and getting ready to check out of our hotel, the J&W Marriott Resort and Spa. I decided my trip would not be complete without a visit to the spa (purely for research purposes, you understand) and so booked a Mayan Copan Style Massage. My masseuse, Nexy, was full-blooded Mayan. To background music of Mayan music (or a close approximation), I was treated not only to a massage but a ritual involving chanting in Mayan, waving of palm branches, and placement of a large Tiger's Eye over my heart. Fortunately I recalled that, unlike the Aztecs, Mayan rituals did not include removal of the heart. This was followed by a very decadent fifty-minute light massage with oils, incense, and flowers thrown in. I felt so relaxed you could have poured me off the table, but I did steel myself for the follow-up including a eucalyptus scented steam room, a wet sauna, followed by ten minutes in a hot then cool Jacuzzi.

Let's just say the subsequent trip home was a very relaxed one!

In Memoriam

Their Names Liveth Forevermore

Betty Dobson

Emma must have wondered at the cause of such grief.
The Great War tried the spirits of millions and costs
countless soldiers their lives—a huge loss, almost impossible
to comprehend at times.

Emily Myra "Emma" (McLellan) Swaine lived most of her life in
Canso, Nova Scotia. As three of her four sons went off to war, she
probably felt a mixture of fear and pride. Young men died in battle.
She knew that. But she couldn't have known the toll the war years
would take on her family.

The first strikes came from an unexpected quarter. Her father died
in early 1915, a month short of his eighty-eighth birthday. A sad
passing, but Angus McLellan had lived a long life and could go to a
well-deserved rest.

The year passed quietly until the Holiday season. Just four days
before Christmas, Emma lost her husband Samuel. He'd recently
celebrated his fifty-third birthday and readily believed he'd see many
more until brought down by heart failure.

The ensuing years brought more suffering to bear on poor Emma.
Her eldest sons Arthur and Roland died in France in 1916.
Benjamin, her youngest boy, shared their fate in 1918. She also lost
her stepfather, a nephew, and her husband's cousin, but nothing
could compare to losing three of her six children.

How relieved she must have felt knowing that she still had her
only remaining son, Edward, and her daughters Margaret and Jessie
to comfort her through it all.

In 1925, the Town of Canso called upon Emma to unveil their new
War Memorial to the town's fallen heroes. The inscription must
have brought fresh tears to her eyes.

"To the Glory of God, and in loving memory of those who made
the supreme sacrifice in the World War, 1914-1918." A list of 23
names followed, but she would have seen only three. "Their names
liveth forevermore."

Emma left Canso five years later, choosing to live on the other side
of the province with her daughter Jessie. She died in 1946, far from
home, but her family laid her to rest in the Canso Baptist Cemetery,
next to her husband and sons—never parted in their hearts.

The names of Arthur, Roland and Benjamin Swaine, along with

thousands more, are also recorded in Books of Remembrance. The six books—First World War, Second World War, Newfoundland, The Korean War, South African War/Nile Expedition, and The Merchant Navy—are physically located in the Peace Tower on Parliament Hill (in Canada's capital city Ottawa) and also available online.

Flags

Michelle Close Mills

For those who gave until it hurt…

A breeze whipped
and snapped the
long flowing line
of billowing
red
white,
and blue...
Each bearing a tag
denoting the name
of one who had
fallen for us.
So we could be home,
in comfort,
in peace,
praying no one
we know will be
among those who fall,
adding their names
to tags in the
long flowing line
representing young lives
that are gone.

Thanksgiving

Tracing Back Thanksgiving Tradition

Mamta Murthy

E ach year, a number of Americans get together with family and friends on Thanksgiving Day to eat turkey and a variety of dishes. Today the holiday spirit in America is symbolized by a grand and rich Thanksgiving meal. A lot of us read about Thanksgiving in our early years and as the time passes, the history and the tradition behind it fade away to the recesses of our mind. A brief recap then is always welcome to help us remember how it all started. At the end, we must remember that Thanksgiving is a bigger concept than just the story of the founding of the Plymouth Plantation; it brings forth the strength and joys of friendship.

In 1620, the Pilgrims, founders of Plymouth, Massachusetts, arrived in America in search of religious freedom. One hundred and two passengers set out for the land on the *Mayflower*. The Pilgrims had a tough time settling in the New Land. The wheat they had carried with them to plant would not grow in the rocky soil. Food shortages coupled with living in dirt shelters took its toll and soon many were dying. Afraid of the Native Americans, the Pilgrims would quietly bury the dead at night so the Native Americans could not see how many were dying. The Pilgrims were in desperate need of help. One day a Native American named Samoset strolled into the village and spoke to them in English. Samoset, along with a fellow Wampanoag named Squanto who knew English well, communicated with the Pilgrims who were glad for any help they could get. Squanto stayed with the Pilgrims for the next few months teaching them survival skills. He taught them how to cultivate corn, beans, and other vegetables; he taught them about poisonous and medical plants, showed how to dig for clams and draw sap from maple trees to make syrups.

Soon enough the Pilgrims were doing much better. The Pilgrims decided to have a thanksgiving feast to celebrate their good fortune. They used to observe thanksgiving feasts in November in England as part of religious obligations for years before coming to Plymouth.

The leader of the Pilgrims, Captain Miles Standish, invited Squanto, Samoset, and other Wampanoag to join them for a celebration. The Native Americans observed six thanksgiving festivals during the year, including a fall harvest festival. The first Thanksgiving was celebrated to give thanks for the harvest. The

Pilgrims, however, found it difficult to feed over ninety Indians so Massasoit, the Native American leader, asked his men to bring food from home. The Pilgrims and the Wampanoag feasted for three whole days. During the three-day Thanksgiving harvest celebration, the food available to the Pilgrims were "corn" (wheat, by the Pilgrims usage of the word), Indian corn, barley, peas, "fowl" or "waterfowl", five deer, fish such as bass and cod, and lots of wild turkey since these were found in great abundance. That's why even today turkey forms an integral part of Thanksgiving meals.

The Pilgrims however did not celebrate Thanksgiving the next year, or any year thereafter. A number of Presidents, including George Washington, made one-time Thanksgiving holidays. In 1827, Mrs. Sarah Hale began lobbying several Presidents for the instatement of Thanksgiving as a national holiday, but her lobbying was unsuccessful until 1863 when Abraham Lincoln finally made it a national holiday.

Now, Thanksgiving is celebrated on the fourth Thursday of November. This was set by President Franklin D. Roosevelt in 1939 (approved by Congress in 1941). Abraham Lincoln had earlier designated the last Thursday in November as Thanksgiving day but it could occasionally end up being the fifth Thursday which was too close to Christmas for businesses so it was changed by President Roosevelt to fourth Thursday of November. The Pilgrims' first Thanksgiving began at some unknown date between September 21 and November 9, very likely in early October. The date of Thanksgiving was probably set by Lincoln to somewhat correlate with the anchoring of the *Mayflower* at Cape Cod, which occurred on November 21, 1620.

The Pilgrims, Wampanoag and Thanksgiving were first linked together in 1841, when historian Alexander Young rediscovered Edward Winslow's letter dated December 12, 1621. It was later published in *Mourt's Relation* (1622).

The First Thanksgiving
Thelly Reahm

Our parents had not socialized with each other since our wedding day in May. Now it was time for Thanksgiving.

The Hyders lived in Pine Valley and the Reahms lived in Vista. We had just bought a house somewhere in between. It was not that the families were hostile, it just wasn't convenient. Although, my parents did have mixed emotions about my taking on the care and feeding of three more children.

The fact that our parent's backgrounds were very similar didn't soothe my nerves any, however they had much in common. Roots in the mid-west, Christian upbringing, survived The Great Depression, long-term marriages to each other, and having only one child each. You would think that entertaining them would be a piece of cake. Not!

I was as frantic as if this Thanksgiving meal was the first one I'd ever cooked for company. I cleaned for a 'white glove inspection'. I read and re-read at least ten articles on how to prepare a fabulous turkey dinner. I was not feeling at all secure.

I wrote down the menu I was going to serve as if Thanksgiving turkey would be hard to forget. I would be serving basically the same menu I'd served in my previous marriage of seventeen years and the same dishes I had eaten for the previous eighteen years I had lived with my parents.

What could go wrong? What could I possibly forget?

I lined all the kids up for inspection before the grandparents arrived. Their faces were clean....hair shampooed. Clothes ironed. Shoes polished. Then one last inspection of their rooms. Everything was fine. Toys picked up. Toilets flushed.

I basted the turkey one more time. The pies were cooling on the teacart. The hors d'oeuvre plates were ready in the refrigerator. The coffee was made, candles were on the table. Sugar and creamer were filled and ready.

"Would you turn the stereo on, Dick?" I called to my husband in the living room.

I heard him get up from his leather chair, but I didn't hear the music, so I peaked around the dining room wall.

"I love you. I love you...." he said to the stereo.

"What are you doing?" I was not seeing anything funny about

this....the Reahms and the Hyders were due any minute and I was getting testy.

"You said to turn it on....and I'm just trying my best....I love you stereo!" he said laughing.

I finally laughed although I was in no mood for his special brand of humour. I realized that he was trying to get me to lighten up a bit.

He flipped the switch and soft music pervaded the room. A great stereo was another addition I got from this marriage, complete with tweeters and woofers. I really enjoyed good music, and he had strung wire to each room during construction so we had an intercom and music everywhere.

The doorbell rang.

Then it was pandemonium with this mixed up brood of kids trying to get un-divided attention from their respective grandparents, but also cutting their new step-sibs out when they could. There was a lot of rivalry going on just under the surface and it kept me edgy most of the time. It seemed there just wasn't enough of me to go around and they were a needy bunch of children.

We all sat down at the dining table, the candles glowing, the food smelling better all the time, and the grandparents oohing and ahhing over all the food I'd prepared. I sighed. I knew now it was going well.

"Poppy, would you ask the blessing?" Dick said.

I placed the golden brown turkey in front of Dick. I sat down at the opposite end of the table and bowed my head. I breathed deeply as my father asked the blessing. It was a moment to centre myself and try to relax. I felt now with everything on the table I could finally enjoy Thanksgiving dinner.

"Will you carve the turkey now, Ben?" I asked sweetly, as I unfolded my napkin and smoothed it on my lap.

Ten sets of eyes rolled up in their heads as they turned to look at me in total dismay.

I froze. My face flamed crimson. I'd really blown it.

The one thing about this Thanksgiving I hadn't remembered was my new husband's name!

Turkey Therapy

Roberta Beach Jacobson

Newly divorced friends should never be abandoned on holidays, and seeing how Nan and I had our divorces well behind us, we were glad to come to the rescue. There would be four of us, girlfriends from high school, thirty-some years down the potholed road of life, slightly used, maybe a bit wrinkled—talking turkey on Thanksgiving.

It would be like transforming the worst of times into the best of times. Nan and I would inspire them, talk them out of the funk that seems to descend upon a woman the first weeks or months after a divorce, when her entire world seems topsy-turvy.

It was our first time preparing a turkey together, but we were a great team. We were confident we could deal with the thawed bird and whip up a splendid feast for our friends in need. Their husbands may have failed them miserably but we wouldn't!

This was a 14-pounder with the works. Nan and I started at 6:30 in the morning. We peeled potatoes, diced onions, chilled the wine, rolled piecrust. I set the table with my best (only) china and Nan's crystal. We stuck to a strict time schedule; otherwise we'd never be ready in time. Our guests were due at 2 p.m., dragging their wounded hearts.

We finished just in time. Two o'clock on the dot. The salad and the pies were in the fridge. The mints were on the table. Everything was elegant, the perfect setting to console two confused souls.

It was 2:30, then 3 p.m. Nobody came. We shrugged. We tested the doorbell. We checked the warming turkey, the dressing, the rolls. At 3:15, I nervously dialled my friends' numbers. Nobody answered at either apartment. So Nan and I waited some more, sampling the dip. Why not just eat while we wait? When we finally carved the turkey, it was getting dark outside. It was far from the special soul-bearing celebration we'd imagined and we were feeling both stood up and let down.

It wasn't until the next day at work that we learned what happened. We'd prepared our grand dinner the Thursday before Thanksgiving!

Excess and Dad's Exes

Linda J. Hutchinson

My favourite holiday meal has always been Thanksgiving supper. As a very young child, that meant an elegant meal, with no violence. As an older child, that meant sharing my Daddy with his current wife and understanding more of the jokes. As an adult I've savoured those memories and chosen carefully which ones to recreate for my children.

At those long-ago family suppers, we gathered around a huge table at my grandparent's home. Jokes flew as fast as the biscuits. Then Gram, Aunt Sara, and I—the ones who had done all the cooking—did all the cleaning up. The same three or four in-laws/out-laws/exes hid out in the bathrooms until the dishes were done, year after year.

Much to my sibling's and my chagrin, our dad had an un-natural proclivity for saying "I do" and seemed t o marry the same woman five times. Only the names, heights, and bra sizes seemed to change. His wives had more traits in common than the Stepford Wives, but one common flaw that drove the whole family to picnic envy was a distaste for helping out in the kitchen. There was usually at least one current wife and one "ex" at the Thanksgiving meal. We were civilized by that time, after all.

One Thanksgiving, Uncle Kenny—family jokester, husband of Aunt Sara, and little brother to our Dad—decided it "was time". As each person arrived Uncle Kenny had them draw out a small folded up piece of paper from a hat and told them there would be a drawing after the meal.

The slackers stood up as soon as the last bite had been swallowed. Uncle Kenny stood up with them and asked everyone to look at their folded paper. He explained the numbers represented a turn to use the "necessary rooms". We all giggled because we knew he had rigged it so that those who always escaped clean-up had very high numbers, meaning they had plenty of time to help out while Gram, Sara, and I enjoyed a cup of coffee, and the use of the bathrooms, in turn, of course.

It would only work once, but at least the chronic offenders, soon red-handed from the hot soapy dishwater, had been put on notice.

Only the names, shapes, and sizes of the slackers changed as the years went by, but we had one more family joke to add to the arsenal.

The Day After Thanksgiving Holiday
E.D. Easley

*I*t was the day after Thanksgiving.
There was a spectacular sunrise. It broke the clouds just high enough for an amazing show with huge, white, fluffy clouds and an explosion of colour.

It's why God gave us LSD. Thousands of rejects from the Sixties and Seventies sat on their porches; ignoring the freezing temperatures and deep snow, sinking deep into flashbacks Timothy Leary had never foreseen.

Each ex-hippy, the ones who are now used-car salesmen, bankers, journalists—hell, mayors–saw something different. It sure beat HBO.

The show stopped after about half an hour—well, for most of them. The folks on Darvocet usually spaced a little longer. This had been a whopper. Overnight a foot of snow was dumped on the Valley—pretty much paralysing everything.

Everybody breathing—except retail employees and the folks working at McDonalds—took the day before off. Because of the snow, the world was supposed to stand still today. But this was America, and this was The Big Event. The only important real estate was blacktop covered with white stuff—and if you wanted to get a parking space within a mile of the Mall, you had to get there Soon. If it was Later, you had to pick over What Was Left.

What Was Left was not pretty at all today.

It was the day of The After Thanksgiving Sales.

All the big games were over. The remaining turkey would become sandwiches for a couple of days…a week if you didn't mind gambling with food poisoning.

You could smell people making hearty breakfasts. It was an opportunity for loving families to get together for another meal, to thank their God for the year's bounty.

Then in other homes you could hear the beer tabs snap and almost smell the Bud. It went down with whatever chips they could find on the floor and the dip the dog hadn't already snarfed. You could hear the kids as they turned on the TV to find whatever was on the Playboy Channel.

It was about then the Mall had a surprise visitor. They came from Above.

It was an unexpected landing—an emergency.

The aliens needed a toilet plunger. Their facilities backed up somewhere around Pluto, and Darf Berkle, the engineer, said the nearest hardware store was on Earth. They had to shut off their faster-than-light drive because they were in a solar system, and a speed limit was in effect—so it had been a really long billion or so miles.

In their culture, it was really bad manners to, well, not use proper facilities.

Wert Lingu was a whiner anyway; it was no wonder why he never made it past radioman's mate. By this point he was seriously complaining.

Once they arrived Tegh Utyb, the captain, ordered the landing. Berkle fired the jets, and they had a smooth touchdown. Captain Utyb slapped him on the fin, congratulating for a great job.

Lingu whined again, and Utyb dropped the hatch so they could get out.

Most roads were snowed in, the rest were slick. So when folks headed for the Mall they should have been doing something else. Like drinking hot cider laced with lots of Bacardi.

Like a foot of snow was going to stop them—from driving, anyway.

They came on foot. They chained up. They played bumper cars on the slick roads, causing millions of dollars of damage to their vehicles, and untold damage to their bodies. But a little whiplash didn't stop them.

About a thousand cars arrived at the Mall. There was room for 500.

"Tow that "f—king thing out of here," yelled Martha, a little old lady hitching a wrinkled old thumb over her shoulder at the starship. "I missed my bingo game to be here today. Then I had to walk half a mile because of this?"

She took her brown cane in both hands, and shoved Mike, the six-foot security guard, against the Mall's glass door. "My Rambler's back there, young fella! Do you know what it's like to walk all that way with arthritis?"

Captain Utyb slithered up just then. He noted how Martha was manhandling Mike. It was just about the time his shipmates slithered up behind him.

"Wow," Derf whistled. "I don't know if we ought to screw with the little one. She must be with the infantry."

"Listen, Captain," Lingu said, "I don't know if I can hold it much longer—you're going to have a mess on your hands—soon!"

Tegh knew he had to act. He adjusted his universal translator and stepped up to the obvious leader, the little old lady.

"Is there a problem here?" Tegh snorted.

"Yeah," Martha replied, shaking her umbrella at Tegh. "Get that damn thing out of here. It's taking up half the parking lot!"

Tegh looked over at his ship. "No problem," he snorted and sniffed. "We just need to use your facilities and borrow a toilet plunger."

Martha looked over at Mike. "You hear that?" she shook her head. "It's an RV. So let them use the bathroom and a plunger. Is that so hard?"

Mike shook his head. "We don't open for ten minutes," he explained. "They'll have to wait."

"Screw you!" Martha poked Mike in the groin with the umbrella, doubling him over. "We need those spaces now!"

Mike relented, gave up, and fiddled with his keys. He swung the door open as they headed for it.

"First door on the left, guys," Mike said with a frown. "There's a plunger in there—go ahead and take it."

A huge crowd had assembled for the After Thanksgiving Sales. They figured the Mall was opening. They surged forward to get in through the single glass door. There were thousands of them—it was a human tide.

The aliens, Mike, Martha, and first dozen shoppers didn't have a chance. They were stomped into unrecognizable pools of mixed DNA.

The ship? With no one to pilot it, you'd think it would be the scientific find of all time.

But as things turned out, the Mall called the mayor's office and reported it. Confused, the mayor called the governor. The governor gave it to the feds. Congress allotted $10 million annually to the Department of the Interior to maintain it.

A blue-ribbon commission, costing another $20 million, decided the city should maintain it as a slide for the city's children.

Congress changed its mind and painted it blue, roped it off, then made it a landmark. They named it after the current president. We had a war going on at the time, so to commemorate it, Congress declared it a national holiday.

That's why we all get the day after Thanksgiving off each year.

Christmas

Always Home

Betty Dobson

I'm pretty lucky when it comes to Christmas, and I don't mean in terms of presents. In forty years, I've never missed spending the Holidays with my parents—lovingly referred to as "the folks."

We moved frequently when I was a kid, so we never had a hometown. When people ask me where I'm from, the most specific answer I can give is "Nova Scotia." But I can always go home. No matter where I choose to live, I know that home is where the folks are.

Someday, though, I'll find out what it means to spend Christmas without them. Bad weather. Conflicting schedules. Or, perish the thought, I get married. Barring all that, I have to accept the fact that my parents won't always be there.

Dad won't string lights along the eaves while Mum bakes shortbread cookies and butter tarts. We won't have to wait for him to finish primping for an hour or more before opening our presents. Or wait to see which gifts garner the coveted "That's nice." Dad's so understated.

Who else but Mum will have to pretend that Dad didn't spill the beans about most of her presents? "You don't need a new <insert product here>. There's nothing wrong with the old one." And she won't turn out another perfectly-timed turkey dinner with all the trimmings. (At least she's seen me learn to love cranberries and sweet potatoes. Now if only I'd learn to cook.)

Dad wants the whole family home for Christmas this year. Imagine a two-bedroom house with a finished basement. Throw in two senior citizens, five thirty- and forty-something siblings, three brave spouses, a foreign boyfriend, five bored children, a pampered cat, and limitless variations on the theme of sibling rivalry.

I wouldn't miss it for the world.

So This is Christmas

Kevin Craig

Tinsel dragged from room to room,
illegal passengers of endless stocking feet.
Eggnog, forgotten, congealed
against the sides of crystal glasses.

The star, sitting askew, still twinkles,
offering hope for new miracles.
Presents, once pristine,
now blown apart in a chaotic storm
of tiny fingers.

Stockings scattered,
their once bulking treasures
strewn across the family room floor.
Explosions in every direction,
The hostile aftermath
of too many Christmas crackers.
Decanters tipped
and candy canes bleeding
into innocent cream carpets.

Aunt Helen sits slumped
in the hungry La-Z-Boy,
reaching sideways
for the last crumbled piece
of dimpled shortbread.

Lady, humiliated by antlers,
sits morosely by the fire
licking her hindquarters.
Dad stands on the front lawn
cursing the fallen plastic Santa,
looking to the chimney
with mingled suspicion and wonder.

Mark sits at the window,
wondering if the red wine
on the lip of Dad's tipped glass
will spill from its shaky perch,
and bleed into the innocent snow,
a mirror to the candy cane mess
being worried over inside.

Holiday Giving
Laurie Corzett

Keep me safe
Keep me warm
Keep me close, away from harm
Give me Hope
Give me Love Give me Peace
Life is good
Life is fun
Life's in love with every one
Give me Peace
Give me Hope Give me Joy!
Merry Christmas
Happy Solstice
Every day of light and play
Every shining holiday
Open up your heart
Make yourself of part
of the living
of the giving
My inner voice sang to me
I give my song to you:
Live in joy Live in peace Live in love

A Time-Honoured Tradition

Andrea MacEachern

Until, recently, I never really understood the purpose of Christmas decorating. I mean, as a child, I took it to mean that Santa would soon be coming to place gifts under my Christmas tree. But as I grew older, the point of this tradition became lost on me. I stopped believing in Santa Clause, gifts became less and less important to me and I didn't have any children. So why did my parents continue this yearly tradition of digging through the basement for decorations that would only return to the cellar in a few weeks. I admit, the ambience of Christmas lights and all the colourful decorations did add a warm cosiness to the house in the dead of winter and a change of scenery for a few weeks. The act of decorating also got the whole family together to help out. With, of course, Bony M's classic Christmas album blaring away, we all pitched in to get that twelve-foot tree standing just perfect. The final touch wasn't the star or angel on top of the tree, but the careful placement of my special ornament that was given to me on my first Christmas. A miniature snoopy in a parachute that spun around! I beamed with pride, when, every year, no fail, my mother always made a special place on the tree for the decorations I hand crafted myself. No matter how hideous they were, they were placed where everyone could see them!

But, somewhere along the line, I lost some of that spark I used to get a couple of weeks before Christmas. As I got older, my thoughts turned away from candy, sweets, presents and Santa and I started to associate Christmas with mall madness, and the realization that the true meaning of Christmas gets lost in the shuffle more and more. Add to this the fact that between the years of 1998 and 2000, Christmas went hand in hand with loss for my family and the true meaning was soured for a time. Three people very dear to me were taken away. My maternal grandmother in May of 1998, my grandfather on Christmas Day, 1999 and my paternal grandmother six days later on New year's day, 2000. It took years for me to realize the significance of these events and the reasons why I should come to terms with them and again see Christmas as a peaceful time of year. The time of year when two very special people were taken away from me. I believe it was significant that they passed at such a peaceful time of year.

But again, Christmas took on another significance when in the year 2001, I moved away to another province. In the weeks approaching Christmas that first year away, I became depressed. I wanted to go home. I wanted to hear Christmas music. I wanted to decorate the tree and eat a home-cooked turkey dinner. Coming to the realization that I wouldn't have any of that in my small basement apartment in a strange, new place far away from home, I vowed to scrounge up the extra money to fly home for Christmas. I arrived home a few days before Christmas Eve, and despite the heartache of a few years before, the holiday spirit was fully intact again. But this time, I didn't wonder about the purpose of it all. They would want us to be happy at this time of year, and keep the traditions of generations past going.

That was the last Christmas the five of us spent together. I returned to my new home away from home with a goal for Christmas 2002; I had to acquire my own decorations, learn how to cook a turkey dinner and incorporate my own traditions with the old and learn to have my own Christmas away from home. I met my goal. Mind you, my decorations were slightly primitive and my cooking resulted in nearly burning the house down even though it was just canned turkey soup and powdered mashed potatoes! My first Christmas tree was quite a sight. My funds were limited that year, so buying one was out of the question. I decided to just decorate the windows and put a few lights up and skip the Christmas tree that year. One night close to Christmas, a few friends came over to watch a movie. Of course, they asked why I didn't have a Christmas tree. I explained my situation and they seemed a bit disheartened, but I didn't think anything of it again, until later that night, long after my guests had departed, there was a knock on my door. There they were with a couple of big garbage bags in tow. When I asked what was in the bags, they promptly dumped the contents onto the floor to display an assortment of items from bottle caps to any other nick knack you can think of. Within an hour, my half-dead houseplant was turned into a magnificent Christmas tree. Well, magnificent might be an overstatement to most people who laid eyes on it! It was, after all, just a houseplant with a weird assortment of objects and old decorations on it! But, to me, it was magnificent! My own Charlie Brown Christmas tree! I will never forget it, and how grateful I was to have such caring and thoughtful friends.

On my own five years now, I have accumulated enough decorations to not have to rely on the kindness of others to supply me with them.

I still live alone, but I have my cat, Jack, to help me put up the decorations. Well, actually he's better at ripping them down and destroying them!

I recently returned home for the first time in over four years. Not much has changed. My parents still put up all their decorations although us kids are all grown and on our own. It was nice to revisit those childhood-like times and remember where all those traditions came from. And they're not dying anytime soon.

December

Roy A. Barnes

Just-cut fir beckons:
I arrive to decorate
-Star above glistens

This tree desires gifts
-Shopping with a list in hand:
Long lines to endure

Time given to bake
-Scent of mince pies and cookies
Pervades the kitchen

December's arrived:
It glides like sleds on packed snow
Towards Christmas Day

Dear Santa
Mary McIntosh

Christmas 2005

Dear Santa Claus,
Do you remember me? In 1933 I was ten years old and lived in Brooklyn with Ma, Pa and Danny in those tenement houses near St. Jude's Catholic Church. Remember, I used to love to flip a stick along its iron railing in the front, and listen to the click-clack noise it made. It sounded just like the church bells that tolled for old Mr. McGillicuddy's funeral. He was the nice man who owned the candy store at the corner. When Pa occasionally gave me a penny, Mr. McGillicuddy would let me take forever choosing between liquorice sticks and jawbreakers. I usually chose jawbreakers, as they lasted all afternoon, but I always hoped they'd have a liquorice flavour.

The Great Depression was on that year, and things were hard for everyone. I never really understood it, but I did know money was scarce. We were lucky, for Pa worked as a night watchman at the office building down the street. However, some of his money went for drinks, and when he came home those nights reeking of whisky, I'd help Ma put him to bed. We all slept in one room, my parents' double bed on one wall, and two cots, one for Danny and one for me, on the other. A blanket was thrown over a rope to divide us.

I used to walk by myself around the city and listen to the

noises it made — the elevated train sounding like an angry lion as it rumbled above me; the shrill whistle of the policeman directing traffic; the screeching brakes of a car turning a corner too fast. I never understood, when I listened to the radio, why Jack Benny or George Burns got such a laugh when they mentioned the word 'Brooklyn.' It was depressing living here during the Depression. Maybe that's what the word meant.

Was it possible the Depression was felt up at the North Pole too? Were you not able to pay the elves that helped you? Was that why you didn't bring me what I asked for that year?

I saw them in the Sears, Roebuck catalogue, and if Sears had them, then I knew you'd have them too.

GENUINE RACER ROLLER SKATES
'Fly like the wind down the pavement'
Only $3.98

That's all I wanted--no dolls, no dresses, no hair bows, just roller skates.

I'm now 81 years old. Sometimes I get confused and forget things, but I do remember that Christmas.

Santa Claus, where are my skates?

Your friend,
Molly Malone

Australian Christmas Holiday

Susan Stephenson

"Oh, cripes, he's off again!"
Tossing my magazine onto the towel, I raced across hot sand to rescue my lemming-like son. His irresistible fascination for the ocean led him to crawling towards it at every opportunity. When picked up and dumped down onto the sand, facing in the opposite direction, he would crawl in a curve until he was heading inexorably for the sea again.

I sometimes wondered if he would continue crawling under the waves until he turned into Underwater Boy. But the Mother in me would kick in before the Scientist could find out.

It was December 1989 and the first day of our Christmas holiday. Waist-deep in the water, I held my son so that his feet swirled through the frothing surf and I echoed his delighted chuckle. Weeks and weeks of lazy summer days stretched before us. I inhaled lungsful of salty, kelp-laced air and felt as free as the gulls swooping overhead.

Back on the shore, we made castles from dribbled wet sand. Higher up on the tide line, sand mosaics made by tiny crabs drew my eyes. Each ball was a perfect sphere placed in patterns I tried to understand. Tim liked to practise walking on them while I held his hands, a gift of crustacean reflexology just for him.

My son yawned and snuggled into my shoulder. We headed back to our special place under the she-oaks, a shady spot for lazing. I tickled Tim's toes with the fine cream sand but he was too content to wriggle them. Warm and salty, his eyelids fluttered closed and he fell asleep on my towel.

Hugging my knees, I gazed out to the dancing horizon. Would my son remember these days of perfection? Fragments of my own childhood summer holidays flickered through my mind. Bubble swimming costumes with a sand-filled crotch; glassy fish scales on crisp brown grass; sandy, cracked linoleum in holiday flats; all with the soundtrack of waves lapping or crashing on the beach.

And the smell? Underlay of seaweed and salt breeze but the overpowering high note of sea creatures decaying in a forgotten pail. My dad taught us to do the pipi twist and from then on, my brother and I must have been responsible for severely depleting pipi stocks along the Australian east coast. We experimented with roast pipi,

pipi stew and pipi fritters but they all resembled leathery fish paste. We much preferred the newspaper-wrapped fish and chips from the shop down the street.

A raucous screech broke my reverie and I looked up to see black cockatoos flying above me. Three—in local lore, that meant rain was coming. I inspected the cloudless, blue sky and mused that it no doubt would rain. Someday.

The screeching woke Tim who smiled up at me. Then he rolled over and started crawling towards the ocean. I laughed and crawled off after him. "Ok, Timmy-boy, let's work on those holiday memories."

Christmas Grows on Trees

Mary Cook

The Christmas tree has its roots firmly entrenched in the soil of pagan times. But Christianity hijacked it in eighth-century Germany when St Boniface swapped the sacred oak of Odin for a decorated fir tree as a symbol of Christmas. Over the centuries it gave rise to various tree-based traditions, which spread throughout Europe.

It's the Victorians who are credited with inventing Christmas as we celebrate it in England today. And almost invariably a decorated fir tree is central to the celebrations.

Christmas trees were not unknown in England from Georgian times. But it was Prince Albert of Saxe-Coberg and Gotha who uprooted it from Germany and planted it in the hearts of the English people. On a visit to England in 1839, Albert brought a tree from his native Germany as a courtship gift to the young Princess Victoria. It apparently worked its magic as the couple married the following year.

So great was Albert's love for the Christmas trees of his childhood homeland that each year he distributed trees to schools and military establishments. And in 1848, the Illustrated London News featured an engraving of the Royal Family around their Christmas tree.

Novelist Charles Dickens took up the theme in his seasonal essay A Christmas Tree, which he wrote in the 1850s for the journal Household Notes. In it he described in minute detail a "pretty German toy"—a tree lavishly decorated and laden with gifts, toys and sweetmeats. And, as one small girl confided to another in the essay: "There was everything, and more."

At the time of year when parents constantly remind children that money doesn't grow on trees, it can reasonably be argued that Christmas does. New traditions surrounding that magical fir tree are being made by ordinary families year by year. Mine is no exception.

When I was a child growing up in post-war England, choosing the tree from our local greengrocer was a very serious business, limited as we were by a shortage of space and a tight budget.

We decorated the tree around the second weekend of December with tinsel, paper lanterns and glass baubles. There were also chocolate novelties and small toys. My brother and I started our celebrations ten days before Christmas, and every evening we were each allowed to choose one item off the tree.

When we were older and my parents grew a little more affluent, the family began to buy more alcohol than the single bottles of sherry and port wine they'd previously allowed themselves with which to celebrate Christmas. For each of the ten days before the big day, we toasted the festive season with a different bottle of wine from under the tree. And although we were too old for toys, my brother and I still insisted on our chocolate novelties!

Every year since 1947 a gigantic Norwegian spruce tree has been set up in Trafalgar Square, London. A gift from the people of Oslo, Norway, it's sent as a mark of gratitude to the English people who harboured King Haakon of Norway when he was exiled by the German occupation of his country during the Second World War.

And every year my mother unearths the artificial Christmas tree she bought in the 1960s. About eight inches tall and constantly battered from being stowed away in a shoebox, it resembles nothing more festive than a bunch of mangled pipe cleaners. But to throw it away would be an unthinkable break with family tradition.

One of my favourite childhood memories dates back to the late 1940s. My family spent Boxing Day, the day after Christmas, with my grandparents who kept a tree laden with small gifts for the entire family. After a festive meal, Grandmother took us to choose a gift from her tree.

It was then that my little brother, no more than two years old at the time, cranked the "everything and more" concept up a gear. Overwhelmed by the vast array of gifts on offer, he stared saucer-eyed at the tree for what seemed like an eternity. Eventually he stuttered: "I want something you haven't got."

Christmas Without You

Michelle V. Pozar

I had always liked this time of year, until now. You were off doing your own thing, and I was at home wishing you were here. This didn't seem like Christmas at all. I always thought Christmas was a time to be with family. You had said you felt the need to be with your family this year. How deluded I've been all these years, I thought that meant me.

Sure, it was nice to spend time with the relatives, but not our special time. We had spent every Christmas together. Why did you have to go and ruin it, our perfect record? I felt special that you had always wanted to be with me on Christmas. Had I done something wrong? Did I disappoint you in some way? Were you getting tired of me? Too many questions begged for answers.

You said I could go with you, but it just wouldn't be the same. I had always thought we had such an equal relationship. I thought we always discussed everything, up until last week. You just walked up to me and announced you were going to spend Christmas with your family. Then added a quick, "Wanna go?" I'm sure you saw the look on my face as it fell to the floor, but you didn't say anything. It happened so quickly I didn't recover until after the crash. Either I was lacking awareness or something had changed.

I looked out the kitchen window and watched the snowflakes fall. I knew if you were here, we'd be getting ready to go shovel snow off the sidewalks and reclaim our buried car. I thought of you driving down to Relic Bay, where your folks lived, and wondered why. I smiled knowing we never would have found the car. Instead, we'd end up building snow people and sledding down by the skating pond. Snow people, my point exactly, it was always equal. It was one of those things we always did, every winter when we went out to shovel that first snow. This was one of the many things I always knew I could count on, our own silly ritual. Why were you changing everything now? Why didn't you want to be with me this year?

Tobias Tinkle, the puppy we had picked out together last Christmas, walked over and looked at me. He had retained the name given him the first time he didn't make it outside. He was also wondering why you weren't here. You were always saying animals knew more than people gave them credit for. "So, what do you know Mr. Tobias?" He looked at the door.

I knew Toby wanted to go play in the snow. He had already been out once, running in circles, barking for me to join him. I just didn't feel like being that happy right now. I'd go fake it with him later. I did open the back door and let him out into the yard again. No sense in everyone being miserable this holiday.

Pouring myself another cup of coffee, I began going over the last couple of months in my head, trying to discover what had brought us to this change. The first time I retraced our recent past nothing seemed out of character for either of us. However, on my second round trip I couldn't believe what I had missed all these weeks. You had started exercising, every week. I knew what that meant! I used to preach to my friends what that meant. If all of a sudden someone started exercising regularly, for no obvious reason, and watching what he ate, something was up. It was the beginning of the end. They were getting ready to make their move, on someone else!

My coffee cup made a loud thud on the table as I set it down like I was squashing a bug. So, that's why you don't care if you're with me this Christmas or not. You found someone else. How could I be so blind? All the signs had been there. Exercising, dieting, being distracted, disinterest in sex. No wonder you didn't include me in your description of family any longer.

When the Christmas song you programmed into the phone rang out, I thought about not answering, but knew I would. It might be you; you said you'd call. I was surprised to hear your sister on the other end. She sounded as if she'd been crying, my heart jumped to my throat.

Then it began. Everything slowed to shock. I heard random words she said here and there, but the message that kept playing over and over was louder than anything I had ever heard before. She had started out with a pleasant enough greeting, and then she had said the words I would never forget. She said she was sorry you were so ill. She told me you had gone there to ask them to be there for me when you no longer could. My world stopped as I grasped for anything to steady me. Was this some sick twisted game she was playing?

I knew it wasn't a game. I knew now why you couldn't be here. You wouldn't want all the wonderful holidays we had shared here to be tarnished. I knew you were thinking of me when you asked your family to watch out for me. I knew it was true because it explained everything. I knew more than anything that I just wanted to be with you. Nothing else mattered now. I wanted you to be well and us to

Christmas Without You   65

be safe. I wanted this to go away. I wanted you to tell me it was a joke as we were making snow people.

Now I wish you were just having an affair. I wish I could share you with everyone. I wish my arms were around you and I could get one of your bear hugs. I'd look into your sparkling eyes and see my reflection loving you. I wished this wasn't going to be the first of many Christmases we wouldn't be here together, but I knew it would.

I hung the phone up and got ready to make the longest trip of my life. We would be together this last Christmas you were outside my heart as well as within. "C'mon Tobias, Daddy needs us."

Winter Solstice

Laurie Corzett

The darkness descends.
As we cry out for warmth and light
Our voices turn to spirit-imbued song
Our frantic movements against the cold
turn to ecstatic dancing.
We take comfort from each other's warmth
and celebrate the life within
struggling to survive.
'Tis the season to relearn the magic
As we share our heavy burdens
of fear and despair.
Joining hands, dancing 'round the fire,
we raise our sight to the sky
and each day,
the days get lighter.

Happy Holidays You Bah-Hum-Buggin' Vamps

Diana M. Hartman

Sung to the tune of "If You're Happy and You Know It"

If you're vandalizin' that Nativity
It's because you're on our private property
If you try to block our Christmas 'cos you think it is your business
The police might find you choking on a wreath

If our Hanukkah upsets you get a life
Our menorah burns despite your civil rights
If you don't like that we're Jewish 'cos you are so bored and ghoulish
You can sit upon our dreidel, spin all night

We're Agnostic and we really like our tree
And beneath it there is no nativity
Still our rights are as protected as you think they are subjective
Happy Holidays, get off my lawn you creep

Winter Solstice brings us from a dreary fog
It's our Sun god's time to hear us sing in togs
If you cloud up our festivities with your boorish incivilities
We might have to smack you with our Yule log

Oh you grinches and your "I'm offended" gruff
We've all banded up together 'gainst your stuff
No it's not unconstitutional, and we've formed a big tribunal
We are here to tell you we have had enough

We are Christian, we are Jewish, and we're proud
We're Agnostic, we're from Druids, hear us loud
We will sing and we will dance and we will seriously prance
You don't get to say we never were allowed

Merry Christmas in your face, here have some ham
Happy Hanukah, be useful, light a lamp
Joyous Yule, you can't stop it, why not go ahead and drop it
Happy Holidays you bah-hum-buggin' vamps

Oy! It's Christmas Again!

Ruth Dickson

I've never made any secret of my contempt for organized religion or the fact that I believe it to be the most heinous concept the human animal has ever perpetrated against itself. The violence, hatred, divisiveness, and self-deception it engenders far outweighs any possible good it does, making religious classification appear to me as the biggest weapon of mass destruction ever conceived.

Nevertheless, I have to admit that the Christmas season is the one time of year I get religion. Starting around December first, I become very, very Jewish. Not that I do menorahs and dreidels, nor am I Grinchy or Scroogey. I just prefer to ignore the whole thing and behave as though Retail Madness is not erupting all around me. The one concession I sometimes make to the ho-ho-ho's is to buy a poinsettia plant after they go on sale. Beyond that, Christmas is the 25th of December, no more or less important than any other day on the calendar.

As for the current debate between "Merry Christmas" and "Happy Holidays", I can only gape in disbelief. Don't these fanatics have any better use for their tiny minds? The two major forces of evil in this country, religion and politics, once again butt heads in their endless fight for dominance of the American belief system. What started as a religious celebration somehow morphed into a federal holiday, so we have still another example of the destruction of the barrier between church and state. So how about we call it "Screw the First Amendment Day" and have done with it.

Anyway, my seasonal wish for you all is to stay warm, stay out of crowds, stay home, and stay sane. And stop sending those damn cards!

Deck the Halls...

Richard Crowhurst

*A*s the song reminds us, this is the time of year when we should "Deck the halls with boughs of holly Fa-la-la-la-la, la-la-la-la." Today few of us fill our houses with evergreen branches of holly, ivy or even yew. Yet, while we still take advantage a hanging sprig of mistletoe to sneak a kiss, or place a holly wreath (whether real of fake) on the front door, few of us are aware of how much folklore surrounds these humble plants.

Traditionally evergreen plants that were destined for use as Christmas decorations were gathered on the Winter Solstice, as it was thought that they would then bring good luck and a long life. Today decorations are generally put up about two weeks before Christmas and it is unlucky for them be left up after Twelfth Night. However, before the twentieth century, it was unlucky for holly and mistletoe to be brought indoors before Christmas Eve, and Holly was thought to be particularly unlucky inside a house outside the Christmas period. In England another belief says that evergreens for Christmas should be delivered by a man, as this will counteract some of the ill luck.

Our ancestors were less concerned with taking their decorations down and it was commonly felt, at least until the Victorian era that evergreens could be safely left in situ until Candlemas Day on 2 February. Woe betides anyone who exceeded this deadline however. One legend from Suffolk in England warned that if a single leaf or berry was left behind in church after the festive period, then the family that occupied the offending pew would suffer a death during the year.

One favourite decoration that dated back to Elizabethan times was the 'kissing bough'; a garland of greenery shaped roughly like a crown and decorated with coloured paper, fruit and candles. These were never hung in their final resting place until they were finished, as that particular hook was sacred to the bough itself. The mistletoe hung in the centre of the garland is still an integral part of Christmas today.

Holly was another popular decoration and the cutting of Christmas boughs is one of the few times that holly, also known as the King's tree, could be cut. A sprig of holly placed in the cow shed over the festive period was supposed to bring good luck and health to the herd. Cows also benefited by being fed the evergreen garlands at the end of the festive period, although one assumes that poisonous plants, such as yew, were carefully excluded from this practice.

Holly also influenced the sexual politics of the household, due to the different male and female strains of the plant. It was thought that both prickly (male) and smooth (female) plants should be included in the decorations so that the family remained harmonious and prosperous in the year to come. It was suggested that the two types should be brought into the house at the same time, as if one preceded the other, then the corresponding member of the household would dominate their partner, something that certain wives in Derbyshire were said to exploit.

The actual plants used for decoration varied widely, with the main criteria being that they provided the necessary greenery. It was often thought that the use of a particular plant in isolation would bring bad luck, or even death, and old country folklore warns against using ivy or yew branches without complimenting them with other plants. Interestingly, the self-imposed ban on mistletoe in church due to its pagan associations with Druidism is something of a recent invention in those parishes where it is enforced.

As a final aside, even some of the edible treats that we regard as traditional today have their origins in plant customs. Today we think of a Yule Log as being a rolled chocolate sponge cake, but it takes its name from a custom that came from the Viking winter festival of light, when bonfires were light across the country. A large log or faggot of Ash was pulled from the forest on Christmas Eve and decorated with ribbons or green twigs. This was the 'Yule Log', that was kept burning throughout the Christmas period. A wish could be made each time one of the bonds snapped and at the end of the holidays a few charred embers would be kept to act as kindling for the following year.

Thirteen Plates

Christine Cristiano

Throughout my childhood years, my life was entwined with traditions that were passed down from generation to generation. Christmas was the most celebrated holiday and it was done so with great Italian flair. Our biggest festivity took place on Christmas Eve celebrated with my father's side of the family. Christmas Eve was called La Vigilia; the night prior to a religion feast is considered a vigil. Of course, being of Italian heritage, food played a vital part of the celebrations.

The day of Christmas Eve was spent preparing our assigned plate to bring to the celebration. Each family brought an entrée to share amongst the numerous aunts, uncles, nieces and nephews. Being Roman Catholic, meat was prohibited on Christmas Eve so the majority of the dishes consisted of fish of one kind or another. Our traditional feast included pasta, fried rapini, fennel with olive oil for dipping, lupini beans, homemade pizza, baccala (salted cod), seafood salad, breaded haddock, fried calamari, and an array of cooked shellfish.

Our traditional tomato pasta sauce was modified for the special event. The soft, pork meatballs were forgone and replaced with small pieces of squid. I remember peering into the large pasta pot while my father stirred the sauce. With each stir, little squid tentacles would poke out of the red sauce. I could see my father's mouth watering at the sight but I could only grimace – to this day I cannot bring myself to eat squid even if it's a delicacy now.

Once nightfall arrived, we would gather at someone's house. The long banquet tables were hauled out of the garage, carried down to the basement and covered with our finest Christmas linens. One by one, all my relatives arrived bearing hot plates of fish, pasta, meatless pizza, vegetables and pastries. My grandmother's contribution, and the family favourite, was her deep-fried Italian donuts. Her donuts were similar to regular donuts but the dough was much heavier and laden with oil that left a shiny layer on your fingers. She only made them at Christmas so they were especially enjoyed by all.

Once everyone arrived, it was time for the counting of plates. In keeping with the readings of the bible, the dining table must consist of thirteen plates bearing thirteen different foods. If by chance, there were less than thirteen dishes, a visit to kitchen was in order to produce another plate for the table. It didn't have to be anything elaborate; a pickle tray peppered with black and green olives would suffice. Although the tradition of thirteen dishes has been passed down through the generations, we never really knew for sure where it started and why. As we grew older, we began to inquire about the thirteen dishes. We learned that a traditional Christmas Eve feast should consist of at least seven fish dishes to represent the Seven Sacraments of the Catholic Church; thirteen dishes represented the Stations of the Cross and also represented Jesus and the Apostles. Coincidentally, thirteen is a lucky number for Italians.

The Christmas Eve celebrations with my father's family have long passed but the traditions still continue with my siblings and myself. Each Christmas Eve, a menu is decided upon and each family brings a dish to contribute to the table. Before Grace is said, the dinner host administers the counting of plates. Evidently, one or more small plates of bread or pickles will be added to the menu for extra good luck and a gesture of thankfulness to the Holy Spirit.

The Christmas Dragon

Gilda V. Bryant

This Christmas, I wanted to play it safe. No muss, no fuss. Sick of rude shoppers, terrified of kamikaze drivers, and disgusted with December holiday sales pitches that started in late October, I longed for something simple.

I wanted to share a carefree Christmas party with my girls. As a Girl Scout leader, was it too much to ask to eat at a respectable restaurant, exchange gifts with my troop, then rush home?

The girls had a different idea. Divided into patrols, the sixth graders planned their Christmas party with creative fervour.

Meagan's group wanted to go to a local Mexican restaurant to eat and exchange gifts. I openly and shamelessly encouraged this idea with the comment, "Enchiladas are delicious and probably good for you." My mouth watered in anticipation of cheese and meat enchiladas, flavoured with just the right amount of cumin and cilantro, served with tostados and salsa, Spanish rice, and beans.

When asked, our more progressive patrol, led by red-haired Bethany told me, "We want to check into the fancy hotel downtown, swim in the heated indoor pool, and have a bunch of room service!" These girls grinned and nodded at each other, as I looked at the scuffed floor thinking of all the reasons this idea wouldn't fly.

As I hemmed and hawed, avoiding eye contact with the swim patrol, the third crew surprised me with their idea. "We have our costumes left over from last year's Christmas play. We want to wear them."

"Do you think you've outgrown your costumes?" I asked, hoping to guide them into constructive, clear thinking.

"No."

"Are Christmas costumes appropriate?" I asked, still wishing to nudge them toward a more conservative goal.

"Yes. We can make it work."

While I digested the notion of a masquerade Christmas party, the last patrol had the idea of singing Christmas carols in a nursing home. Rachel pointed out, "Everyone needs a grandma. We can eat enchiladas another time and we'll swim next summer."

We threw ideas around for thirty minutes, which only seemed like a week. I continued to remind the girls how delicious hot enchiladas could be on a cold winter's night.

After a much-heated discussion, and even some cajoling and whining from me, the party plans were complete. Although not quite satisfied with the results, I promised to make the necessary arrangements.

I met the girls in the nursing home parking lot on the day of the party to count heads, issue lyrics of Christmas carols, and give last minute instructions and threats.

Then, their amazing costumes caught my attention. Two or three girls wore their official Girl Scout uniforms with the unofficial addition of fuzzy red Santa hats. Several girls displayed bright cheery Christmas sweaters. One blond Mrs. Santa, complete with bonnet, long red dress, apron, and wire granny glasses grinned the entire visit. One child, an elf with enormous padded crimson feet, jingled whenever she took a step or a breath. We had our own blue-eyed Christmas tree—complete with ornaments.

I had to look twice at the last two girls. A short lime-green polyester dragon brought up the rear with a much taller scout, regally holding the tail as if it were an elaborate train of a glorious wedding dress. The dragon's green head had eyes with moving parts and white felt teeth that wiggled when she exhaled. Bright yellow scales poked out along the dragon's back. Red sneakers completed the outfit.

"Who's the green dragon?" I asked the elf.

"Oh, that's Rachel. Remember, she told us 'Everyone needs a grandma.'?"

Smiling, I realized I had never heard of the Christmas Dragon, but she encompassed and promoted the ideals of the Christmas spirit. She was cheerful, reverent, loving and probably thrifty and brave too.

We entered the nursing home, noisily trooping through the spotless, shining halls that held a slight ambience of disinfectant. The girls tried to be quiet with loud whispers, giggles, and noisy tiptoeing. The elf's swollen red shoes led the pack with bells jingling.

As we sang, the girls mainly stayed on key, and only strayed once from the traditional Christmas singing by transforming "We Three Kings" into a round. No one seemed to mind that we sang that one over.

In the Alzheimer Unit, some elderly folks kept time with their feet. One white-haired lady transformed into an animated bandleader, perhaps remembering other choirs and music, directing us in four-four time with her hands. Some individuals heard the music and traveled from their rooms by wheelchair to see the commotion.

The residents said, "Girls in costumes? At Christmas? Well, I never. It's about time someone added a little life to this place!"

Grinning residents watched the lime-green polyester dragon share her green, toothy head with a girl wearing the more sedate sensible civilian clothing of skirt and blouse.

Before we left, the girls gave a "Merry Christmas" hug or handshake to each person. Everyone, whether they were in costume, bound to a wheelchair, or nurses on duty, enjoyed the festive experience. A light snow fell as we said our good-byes to residents, other visitors and employees.

En route to the pizza parlour, our girls agreed this was the best Christmas Party we had ever had. I found myself content to eat enchiladas some other time.

I had forgotten the spirit of Christmas calls us to love and care for others. The girls could have had a party strictly for themselves, but they decided they would share some little spark of their loving, caring personalities, costumed, uniformed, or in civilian clothes with lonely, elderly shut-ins. This was their idea; the plan they put into action with my reluctant approval. They embodied the Christmas Spirit-especially the lime-green polyester dragon. I was humbled and proud that my girls reminded me what Christmas could be and should be.

As we left the restaurant, I overheard their eager voices, making plans for another costume-carolling party. I'm even looking forward to next Christmas myself.

Christmas trees enthralled in light

Laurie Corzett

Christmas trees enthralled in light
Bright red and green displays
Shop windows adorned in frosty scenes
Concerts, Carols, Plays
Santa's sleigh displayed on lawns
and rooftops
Holly! Mistletoe!
Christmas cards arrive each day
with memories of long ago.
Welcome to another season's
greetings, parties, gifts and cheer
Make it wonderful; make it grand!
For you and all whom you hold dear—
Merry Christmas, once again;
And dreams of peace for the new year.

A Dash of Cinnamon, a Pinch of the Past, a Smidgen of the Future

Kristin Johnson

Close your eyes and remember December, the smell of cinnamon in your mother's or grandmother's kitchen and the warm scent of dough baking in the oven. Imagine opening the oven door and, with assistance, taking out the heated cookie sheet. Devour the cookies, small works of art, with your eyes: Fudge Brownies, Gingerbread, Nut Rolls, Painted Cookies, Sugar Cookies... With each bite, taste your childhood and family history. You can trace your blood and traditions not by DNA, genealogies and family heirlooms, but by recipes given from one generation to the next, like oral histories handed down in clans before recorded fact caught on.

Scholars once sniffed at "women's lore," but the notations of "1 dash nutmeg" and "1 cup chopped nuts," when handwritten on a yellowing page, are as important to memorize as the dates of the American Revolution. They are a tangible reminder of love, care and craft in any society, but particularly in America, where encouragement to eat bags of artificially sweetened store-bought Christmas sweets leave people sugar-craving, guilty, physically and emotionally empty Christmas cookies are the opposite of this trend. They represent home, family, comfort, joy, and tradition.

It's a miraculous event when generations gather around the stove to spend a day together, getting their hands dirty and sharing of themselves. It is miraculous because those memories are irreplaceable. It's miraculous because children get curious and ask, for example, "Why are the Christmas cookies German? What was Christmas like when you were my age? Did Santa Claus visit you?"

Mother, father, grandmother, and grandfather can share with children the family history and everyday moments in the past, such as, "Your grandmother made a mistake and measured one cup of walnuts when the recipe called for half a cup. But the cookies tasted better, so to this day we always use 1 cup of walnuts in the recipe." By reliving these rare glimpses of a life you may have forgotten, you honour and celebrate yourself as well as your family. Christmas cookies themselves transmit and record history and tradition.

In addition, Christmas cookies are a thread to Christmas past, not only our past, but long past. The word cookie came about thanks to Dutch settlers in North America during the 1700s to 1900s. Koek is

Dutch for cake, so koekje, later cookie in English, means "little cake." Christmas cookies like German Springerle continue the custom of serving Christmas baked goods started by the Romans, Teutonic/Germanic tribes, and other pre-Christian civilizations. Christian religions sanctified these symbols of worship of the harvest gods by adding a "J" on the top to mark the breads as offerings to Jesus Christ. Ancient European peoples ate gingerbread at Winter Solstice feasts. When you bake gingerbread and Springerle, you're participating in a tradition that endures.

In that spirit, here is a recipe for successful cookie making:

Start with 1 family, 1 kitchen, and a box of recipes. Add an uninterrupted period of time. Subtract phone calls, televisions, or any other distractions. For best results, add the Prayer Before Baking from CHRISTMAS COOKIES ARE FOR GIVING:

"God bless this mixture with the sweetest and tastiest ingredients: joy, faith, family, friendship, love, and health. Let the scent of this holiday offering rise to Heaven and make the angels sing, for the happiness of mankind is their feast. Let us taste our blessings with each bite as we share the company of our loved ones. Amen."

Sprinkle with laughter. Add amusing family stories with a lavish hand. Fold in 1 cup patience and understanding, blended with 1 gallon youthful enthusiasm and a pinch of baking know-how. Eat your mistakes with joy. Bake lovingly and well. Enjoy warm, delicious, Christmas miracle cookie-baking memories for years to come!

Our Little Floozy

Gary R. Hoffman

"You really think you can do that?"

My new wife winked at me. "Hey, baby, I can do anything I set my mind to do."

I always figured marriages went through several different stages. We were in that first stage, the one where our apartment was graciously decorated with furniture and accessories from the Goodwill Collection of Mismatched and Assorted Memorabilia. Granted, we had both been married before, but left those unions with what few cloths we could carry. We both had children who were living with us—Mindy had a girl, and I had a boy—and our first Christmas together was approaching. Since neither one of our parents were totally into the fact that we wanted to get married, we moved some distance away from them and decided to set up our own housekeeping.

Now we were trying to figure out how we could decorate for Christmas and still have money left to buy the kids some presents. We cut a cedar tree from along a back road for our Christmas tree. We may have the only "hot" tree in the county. When I was growing up, our Christmas trees always had an angel on top. To me, it just wasn't Christmas without that angel on the tree. We priced some, but they were out of the question. Now, Mindy decided she could make one.

"I've got all kinds of scraps of material and other stuff in my craft box at home. Let's just buy a cheap doll, and I'll make an angel." We found a pre-packaged plastic doll in some variety store, probably costing in the range of forty-nine cents. As Mindy started to create an angel, the kids and I went to work on the tree. One of the first things I did was to cut down the branch in the top-middle so the angel would set there. Within an hour, Mindy came in carrying our new angel. It was really quite beautiful. She had on a white dress, with white netting over it. Mindy had sprinkled some glitter on the dress. Her halo was a sparkly silver pipe cleaner. Her wings were made of white cardboard and edged with silver rick rack.

It was now time to mount our "topper" on the tree. As I remembered the one from my childhood, there was a tube under the angel's dress so she would slip over the top branch. Our new little angel had no tube, but two legs. We decided we could wrap Scotch tape around her legs and the top branch would go between her legs. For some reason, both Mindy and I then realized for the first time our little angel was wearing moulded-on, and painted on, red high heels! We both laughed about having a "floozy" for an angel, but she still looked good on our tree.

Every year from then on, our little floozy brightened our Christmas. In a later stage of our marriage, where we actually did have furniture that matched and looked decent, and we could have easily gone out and bought a new angel, our little gal with the red high heels went on our tree. She was a reminder of a past we would never forget, but also of the love we shared on that first Christmas together.

Christmas Alight

Diana M. Hartman

*I*n 1966 there were a good many stuffed toys made that were flammable. I don't know when they started making them or when they stopped making them. I only remember the impact this had on my wee life and how one remarkable woman saved that day for me many years later.

My Great Grandmother had come to Wichita from Ottawa to spend Christmas day with us. Like all the women from both sides of our family, she was energetic and chatty no matter her age. She'd come with my Grandfather and his wife, Glenna, from Overland Park. The glorious sight of their car in the drive with all those gifts in the back was second only to the tree come Christmas morning. They had arrived in the dark in the middle of a snow shower. It might have been late at night, or it might have been 6:00 in the evening. For some reason I recall their arrival from the vantage point of the front yard rather than through the front window. I watched as my Grandfather and Father piled presents up and took them into the house. The large colourful bulbs that lined the roof were hazy and wondrous through the veil of snowfall. Our tree could be seen through the window. The tinsel didn't hang as much as hover over and around the lights and ornaments. My mother's approach to decorating the tree was nothing less than artistic. A painter, and later a sculptor, she crafted the tree from the inside out with balance, colour, light, and harmony.

The two-bedroom house my parents had rented from my Grandmother was cozy and warm. Our heat came from a floor furnace located in the centre of the house between all the rooms. It was easy enough to avoid even though it was large because it was so hot. It was so hot it was scary. And yet, the bedrooms always held a chill. The cracked windowpanes may have had something to do with that.

The air of Christmas morning was heavy with the smell of bacon and coffee. I stumbled sleepily into the living room with my three brothers, one older and two younger than me. Once the tree was within our sight, we were wide-awake. The presents brought from out of town had been placed under the tree right away, but Mom and Dad always waited until the middle of the night to place theirs. Our patience was rewarded every year with a morning vision so breathtaking I can still see it whenever I close my eyes. Mom gave as much care to how the gifts were arranged as she did the decorating of the tree. The gifts were never stacked or piled. They were their own landscape with depth, shape, and texture whether it was a lean year or a time of abundance. While I fidgeted with anticipation, I was also in no hurry to see the earth of gifts supporting the tree get taken apart. We could always tell what was from Santa because the presents from him were different from all the rest. His came in plain collared paper with no ribbon or bow, just a simple tag with a child's name and signed "Love, Santa." He dutifully left behind crumbs on the cookie plate, a drop or two of milk in the glass, and a note that reminded us of the good things we'd done that year.

After a seemingly endless morning meal, the big people announced it was time to open gifts. This too would require patience as gifts were opened one at a time. My brothers and I were jumpy, clapping at the opening of each gift, not because what someone else received was so great, but because each gift opened put us that much closer to our own. Finally my turn came. Around the room it went, and it was my turn again. And then again. And then one more time. This last package, from Grandpa and Glenna, was as big as I was. I trembled to think what it could be. I was encouraged to peel the paper away slowly but I couldn't hold back. Suddenly, there she was! I was 4 years old and the ever so happy recipient of an Eskimo doll every bit as tall as me. She wore a fuzzy hooded parka, fuzzy mukluks, and a plastic face. A hint of jet-black hair was painted across her forehead. She was beautiful. She was exotic. And she was flammable.

Grandpa took Great-Grandma and Glenna back home early the next day. Other relatives had come for another dinner. During dinner, my brother noticed a fire truck in the neighbourhood. Its lights were flashing but there was no siren. It moved down the street slowly. Firemen were going door to door. And then they came to our house. There was mumbling and an offer of coffee. I was told to bring my Eskimo doll to the table. One of the firemen plucked a bit of fur from the hood of my doll's parka. He laid it in an ashtray and put a match to it. The fur became instantly alight and disappeared. I held my doll tightly. There was more mumbling; something about the floor furnace, and then my heart sank. The firemen took my Eskimo doll with them.

My parents didn't tell my Grandfather and Glenna about this until their Christmas visit in 1980. By then we'd moved across town into a bigger house. Grandpa said he wished he'd have known about the firemen and the doll but thought I was too grown for a replacement. Glenna took me aside later and said she wished she could replace it, that she didn't think anyone could be too grown for a doll they'd had for such a short time. During that same conversation she asked me about my interests and I told her how much I liked to write. After Christmas day dinner I retreated upstairs to my bedroom with an armful of wonderful things. Glenna came up later with a bag. It held a package of pens and several notebooks. If this were a chicken soup story, I would talk about Glenna encouraging me to write about that fateful Christmas day. But this is my story. Glenna looked into my eyes, cupped my face in her hands, and said nothing. My heart swelled every bit as much as it had sank so many years ago.

My grandfather's second wife, Glenna was my grandmother's adversary from day one. While the rest of the family tolerated her, I thought "Glenna" was French for "Grandma" until I was almost a teenager. I only then learned Grandpa had left my Grandmother with two small children in 1950. Grandpa and Glenna married just before I was born in 1962. By the time I found out about all this, it was too late for me not to like her. I loved her.

I knew it was a sappy thing to do but I couldn't help myself. After my Grandfather died, and knowing she was getting on in years herself, I sent her a little Eskimo girl figurine with a card telling her how much she meant to me. She died at home shortly thereafter. I lived far from home when both she and Grandpa had died so I wasn't able to make it back for either funeral. My sister-in-law, who had also held Glenna in high esteem, told me later said she couldn't find the doll. We both agreed this was odd since Glenna kept tedious records and was an avid collector of all things dealing with family. The doll came in my mailbox a few weeks after her funeral with no return address, no card, and postmarked from Anchorage. My sister-in-law insisted she hadn't sent it. I'll probably never know how I came to get it back, but it wouldn't surprise me to find out Heaven's gates are in Alaska.

Christmas in Miramichi
Kevin Craig

The river all but freezes, its brown, choppy middle,
refusing to give in to the demands of science,
continues with the in and out rhythm of its lunar breathing.
The house, an impossible hill away from the rocky shore,
sits in all of its grey and white splendour,
refusing the tawdry decorations of the chintzy Christmas season.

This is the Miramichi, a place of its own,
filled with the festive twinkle
of a season made for its country charms,
yet ignorant of the gaudy blue lights
dangling from the skeletal eaves of homes
back in Toronto's boxed-in sub-divisions.

Trees here, filled with popcorn strands
and cranberry sweetness,
still smell like trees, still bleed a mess of needles,
objects of scorn for rural housewives,
pleasant reminders of a different world
for visiting urban relations.

On Christmas morning, an actual lump of coal,
wrapped safely within pastel-coloured tissue papers,
nestles beside fresh tangerines,
in a stocking hanging from a real mantel.
More reminders of a Christmas away from home,
in the heart of the family's beginnings.

Memories now, these Miramichi Christmases,
in the home of grandparents now expired.
How to explain them to my own children,
expectant of digital wonders in their neon stockings,
which hang from gaudy baubles off the hearth
of a gas fireplace, found within in a boxed-in
sub-division far from the Miramichi's rocky shore?

Luminarias

Krys Douglas

I have no family left in the town where I live; they are all hundreds of miles away in the cold and ice of the Midwest or New England. For the past few years I've spent Christmas Eve with friends. One of their traditions is to visit one of the cemeteries in town. My mother and I often did the same, although not so regularly as to be called a tradition. It's a strange thing, you may think, but New Mexican cemeteries hold a miracle that has no equivalent I've ever come across elsewhere. That's the Luminarias.

Luminarias are small paper bags, the size you use for your school lunch, which contain two or three inches of sand in the bottom. A votive candle is placed in the middle of the sand, and, when it's lit, casts a soft, yellow glow. These are placed on rooftops, sidewalks, and fences, traditionally on Christmas Eve. They are intended to light the way of the Christ child to the homes of the devoted. Of course, these days, there are electric ones that burn continuously from December 1 to January 2. But tradition has them only lit on Christmas and New Year's eves. A side note: there is disagreement over what they should be called. Most people refer to them as luminarias, but in northern New Mexico they are called faralitos, because, in the days before paper bags, people built small bonfires along paths.

In many of the cemeteries, families will take luminarias to the graves and light them Christmas eve. The effect of the thousands of luminarias is of a sea of golden light spread across acres of land. The cemetery my friends and I go to is one of the oldest, and is on a long slope. When you stand at the crest, you can see the entire cemetery spread out, and the glow fills the soul with joy. Yes, there are the incredibly poignant scenes: the teddy bears left at the graves of children, a sign on the grave of a teenager, buried the previous summer, asking Santa to stop here. However, the over-riding effect is of peace and joy in the coming of Christ.

Hurrah the Saturnalia!

Laurie Corzett

Hurrah the Saturnalia!
Bacchus reigns on high
And all the world's a feast of fun
So pass the pipe and pour the rum
And flash a smile o'er everyone
A twinkle of the eye.
Hail the merry Season!
A boost for love & joy
When packages that yell "surprise!"
May dance before our merry eyes
from "Santa Claus" that merry, wise
& venerable old boy.
Joy to all ye revellers!
It's time to join in play
where roles are dropped and laughter raised
We're all buffoons, so clowns be praised
It's time to shout out loud, ablaze
"Joy to all today!"
A very merry holiday
to each and all I say!

Reflections from Shadow[*]

Malcolm Watts

L arge snowflakes settled onto the boys' tongues when they gazed up into the sky. Christmas would arrive in three weeks, and the family was out on a Sunday afternoon to find a tree.

Dad pulled the toboggan and Elizabeth, hands behind her back, walked alongside him. The couple gazed at one another, then the boys, and smiled in the manner of parents captivated with most anything their children did.

A few minutes later, Jared spied a prospective conifer. "Here's one?"

"I think we'll walk a bit until we get to an area where the trees haven't been picked over," Dad said.

Jared wondered what "picked over" meant. Shortly Dad stopped, let go of the towrope, and looked around at the boys. Jared wondered why they had stopped.

"Jared, how about you walk for a bit?"

The sun and mild temperature had made the snow wet, and pulling them proved more work than James anticipated. Jared clamped onto the ropes running down the sides of the toboggan and began yelling.

"NO! I want a ride with Derek."

"Daddy is tired." Mom took him by the hand and pulled him to his feet. "You walk with me a bit; you can see the trees better if you're standing up." She pulled two candy canes from her pocket and handed one to each of the boys. Jared had it in his mouth before Derek could remove his mitt.

"Ummmm. Peppermint." Jared's favourite, next to chocolate.

Mom unwrapped Derek's and handed it back to him.

"Where's mine?" James asked.

"Sorry," Elizabeth replied. "I brought enough for the boys, only."

Families and groups of young people laughed and shouted as they wandered about the tree farm. A group of teenage guys made snowballs then chased their girlfriends around the trees. The girls shrieked with a combination of excitement and annoyance until finally, one girl bent down and scooped some ammunition of her own. Shortly all the girls gave a good account of themselves.

"What kind of tree were you thinking of, Beth?" James asked.

He didn't sound as if he cared. He had learned to leave such decisions

---

[*] An excerpt (chapter six) from the novel of the same name (ISBN 141201419-0).

to his wife; then he didn't have to take the blame or feel responsible for her grumbling if something went wrong.

"I don't know James, probably one with soft needles so the guys won't get hurt when we decorate it. Maybe Balsam?"

"Whatever you say, Beth." James smiled and nodded.

After twenty minutes of walking, the family reached the back of the farm where the trees grew closer together and the groups of people were farther apart.

"There's a nice one, Jared," Mom said, pointing.

Jared broke away from Mom's hand to see the tree in question. Partially blocked from view behind two other trees, it almost seemed skulking to avoid detection.

"How about this one, James?" The six-foot Balsam exuded a distinctly seasonal fragrance.

"I like it!" Jared began jumping up and down. Derek joined him and they chased one another around the tree.

"Well, what do you think, James?" Beth asked.

"It might prove a chore to stand up." James face appeared uncertain as he studied the tree's crooked stem. "Guess it'll be fine."

He pulled a small bucksaw from his pack, locked its jagged blade into business position, then knelt on the toboggan to keep himself dry as he made the cut.

"I want to' help." Jared said.

"All right, but we have to do it together." James took a breath, then sighed. "This saw is very sharp."

James placed his hand over Jared's and they began. Despite their best joint effort, the sawing motion proved awkward.

"I want to stop," Jared said, withdrawing his hand.

James quickly completed the cut on his own before Derek thought to ask for a turn helping. Elizabeth and the boys grabbed the tottering tree and lowered it onto the toboggan. The wind had picked up and the temperature had dropped.

"Let's head back and get some hot chocolate," Elizabeth said.

"Yeah," the boys cheered.

Mom and Derek strolled on ahead while Jared stayed behind to help Dad pull the toboggan. After a short distance, Jared let go of the rope and stepped away to watch the tree slide by. He started to whimper. James looked over to see the troubled look on his face.

"What's wrong, son? Too tired to walk?"

Jared shook his head, then looked up at his dad with a pleading expression.

"When Christmas is done can we put the tree back where it was?"

"No, I'm sorry Jared, but once a tree is cut . . . well, that's it."

"You mean it's dead!' Jared panicked and started crying. He snatched Dad's sleeve and pulled it hard. " Put it back, Dad. Put it back now. Maybe it won't be dead."

James crouched down to Jared's level.

"Sorry Jared. No can do."

Elizabeth had turned around to look.

"What's wrong?" she called.

"Under control, Beth. I'm handling it. Come here Jared." James pulled his son towards him and sat him on his knee. "Jared, these trees here are specially grown for Christmas by the people who own this farm. Next summer they'll plant a baby tree for every one that's cut."

Jared seemed unmoved by this logic, his attention focused on this particular tree's plight, his stare convicting Dad of herbicide.

"C'mon big guy, we've got to go now."

James took Jared's hand, and they walked along in silence. Jared swiped at his face with his mitten as he tried to comprehend this sudden glimpse into the circle of life and death that apparently never stopped.

Even during the happiest time of the year.

Boxing Day at the North Pole
Betty Dobson

underneath the mistletoe
one unattended elf
sipped a cup of day-old cheer
secretly practiced his pucker
and winked at the boss's wife

Peace On Earth…and In Your Home, Too

13 Tips For Holiday Marriage Survival from Couples Married 50+ Years
Sheryl Kurland

*I*t's a holly, jolly time of year! *Screeeeeeeeeeeech!!!* Piggybacking the traditional festivities of the season is the traditional stress the season puts on marriages. While the latter part of the year traditionally provides cue to mental health professionals to issue their conventional lists of marriage advice for surviving the holiday season, couples married 50 years or longer have a different set of guidelines. Having endured decades of family feasts, party roulette, shopping marathons, home decorating and un-decorating, these couples hold the "real-life" formula for marital bliss during the holidays. Espousing experience over analysis, they delightedly reveal their secrets for peace on earth…starting in the home:

1. Never discuss sensitive subjects when you're hungry.

2. Make a list of what not to talk about at family gatherings. Examples: Never use the word "older," as in "Aunt Mary is 'older' than Aunt Susan" or "For an 'older' man, Uncle Harold has a lot of hair." Also, never compare today with the "good ol' days."

3. If there are two ways to interpret what somebody said and one makes you mad and the other doesn't, pick the one that doesn't.

4. Don't talk politics, religion, baseball or football, especially what teams are playing each other in Bowl games.

5. At family dinners, if you've lost weight recently, don't mention it. In fact, wear baggy clothes to make yourself inconspicuous.

6. Never roll your eyes or shush someone's annoying child running around or whining.

7. Take a vacation, i.e., go on a cruise, stay at a bed & breakfast. (If some relatives are insulted by your plan, they're probably the same ones that made you miserable!)

8. Consolidate tasks. Example: Take a nap together. This allows you to accomplish two goals at once: 1) Devote time solely to each other, and 2) Prevent exhaustion.

9. Make dreaded tasks more enjoyable. Example: Chat on the

phone while wrapping presents or addressing holiday cards.

10. Celebrate somebody else's holiday. Forego the lavish, overindulgent holiday feast and, instead, volunteer at a local church, food bank or homeless shelter to help the less fortunate.

11. If an issue arises, decide how big a deal it really is to the two of you – not Aunt Emma or Uncle Fester. And, in the heat of battle, seize fire. And, weather turbulence with laughter.

12. Forget the Norman Rockwell ideal. The piecrust won't be perfect. Scale down your expectations, and focus on what's right rather than what's wrong.

13. An occasional cocktail from time to time helps!

Joyful Noise
Mary Cook

Christmas time is here again
Bringing raucous drunken sounds
Let us sing a loud refrain
Proving festive joy abounds.

Deck the halls with boughs of holly—
Look—our mate has just been decked!
Hoots of George and bawls of Wally
Mean our carol's truly wrecked.

I can stand the church bells ringing
As we bellow yuletide cheer,
But reward our carol singing!
Merry Christmas—where's the beer?

Hanukah

Hanukah Harry

Janet Caplan

For those unfamiliar with it, here's a brief explanation of Hanukah, the Festival of Lights. About 2300 years ago, war broke out between the Maccabees of Israel and the Syrians. The Syrian king, Antiochus, had commanded the Jewish people to reject their customs and beliefs and to worship, instead, the Greek gods. The Maccabees were finally successful after 3 years of fighting and they reclaimed the Temple in Jerusalem. After rededicating the Temple, they wished to kindle the eternal light, but saw that they had enough oil for only one night. A miracle occurred and this oil lasted for eight days, not just one. The victory and rededication are commemorated the world over by Jews when they light the menorah (a special candelabra) each night during the eight days of Hanukah, which falls yearly anywhere between late November and December. Aside from lighting the menorah, gifts are exchanged, games are played with dreidels and special foods such as latkes (potato pancakes) are eaten. It is a joyful and festive time.

Those are the basics: then there's Hanukah Harry, my family's personal guide to the holiday. Harry first appeared when my daughters, Emma and Katie, were about four and two respectively. As with most families, traditions arise around holidays, and being Jewish means having a variety of holidays with which to work. Let's see. Back in Toronto, Passover would be split between our house on one night and one of my brothers' on the second. Rosh Hashanah meant one night at each of my brothers' homes (we got off easy here) and then we would host the Hanukah party. Since my parents still lived in Montreal at the time, the party would consist of our three families—twelve or thirteen of us depending on the year. Well, dozens of latkes were fried, smoked meats and herring were laid out on serving platters, salad piled into bowls and kosher dills and Cole slaw set out as garnishes. I can't forget the desserts either; cookies, cakes, maybe a pie. Food for an army. Once that was all set, the next step was for all of us to gather together in the living room and await Hanukah Harry. His special chair was centred in the room and all of the children would arrange themselves around it, anticipating Harry's imminent arrival.

Okay, so here he comes. Picture a two hundred pound Marx brother look-alike, looking alike by virtue of the fact that he wore a black Harpo style wig and a Groucho eyeglass, nose and moustache mask. He schlepped a large Santa style sack (Harry, always the egalitarian), which was, of course, full of Harry's Hanukah presents. Omigod, the air of expectation, the giggles reverberating in the room. It was all too much for the entire group as Harry pulled the outrageously and beautifully decorated gifts for us all, from his bag. Each presentation required Harry to make a lengthy, humorous, yet personal speech about the recipient. Laughter followed and all in all, a good hour and a half was necessary to complete Harry's mission.

Our Hanukah Harry tradition carried on for about six years in Toronto and was followed by his visitations in Edmonton for another couple of years. I guess that Harry went the way of Santa but we all still talk about him with great fondness and laugh at the wonderful memories created by my husband, Hanukah Harry.

Miracle

Jacqueline Seewald

Cruel conqueror, Antiochus Epiphanes, King of the Syrian-Greeks,
bringer of battle and bloodshed to Israel,
decreed Greek culture take the Torah's place
and Jews worship in pagan idolatry.
Chanah and her seven sons faced death to disobey.
Mattisyahu and his five sons led a rebellion unafraid.
"Whoever is for G-d, let him come to me!" the Kohen cried.
The small Maccabee army outnumbered many times
performed miracles against Greek might.
Swifter than the eagle, mightier than the lion,
Judah led the faithful to victory in the fight.
On they marched to climb the mountain
to restore the Temple to the Holy City.
"If I forget thee O Jerusalem,
May my right hand lose its cunning!"
Through the ruins they rummaged to find
one cask of pure olive oil undefiled.
They poured it into a menorah they put together.
The flame burned true and bright
like the courage of their brave souls,
not for but one day, not for just one night,
the miracle of Chanukah, the eight day Festival of Light.

Author Bios

Roy A. Barnes writes from the plains of Southeastern Wyoming. His poetry and prose have appeared in *InkSpotter News, Heritage Writer, Skive Magazine, Poesia, C/Oasis, The First Line,* and *Skatefic.com.*

Roberta Beach Jacobson is a kid at heart. At twenty-one, she left Chicagoland to explore Europe. After two decades of travelling, she settled on the isolated Greek island of Karpathos, where she spins words and feeds cats. Her Blog is youtrue.blogspot.com and her website is www.travelwriters.com/Roberta.

Gilda V. Bryant is a full-time freelance writer based in Amarillo, Texas. She has worked with children and young people in Boy Scouts, Girl Scouts, Boy Scout Venture Crew, and Boy Scout Explorer Post. Her articles for or about young people have appeared in *Hopscotch, Boys' Life, Youth Educator,* and *Youth and Christian Education.*

George Burden is a family physician who practices in Elmsdale, Nova Scotia. He is also a freelance journalist who has written for *Readers Digest, Funny Times, Stitches, The Medical Post, Ancient Egypt,* and many other publications. He serves on the advisory board of *The Medical Post* and holds the Atlantic Canada/Quebec regional chair for the Manhattan based Explorers Club. Dr. Burden is also co-author of the book *Amazing Medical Stories* (Goose Lane Editions/University of Toronto Press, April 2003).

Janet Caplan lives near Victoria, British Columbia. In addition to her work as an accountant, Janet enjoys writing personal essays, her local writing group and book club, and long boat rowing. Janet and her husband, both from Montreal, have lived in several major Canadian cities through their 36-year marriage and now happily reside with their two dogs, and occasionally one or both of their daughters, in the beautiful town of Sooke on Vancouver Island.

Michelle Close Mills' work has appeared in magazines such as *GreenPrints the Weeder's Digest, Fate,* and *Skyline,* as well as anthologies *Chicken Soup for the Recovering Soul Daily Inspirations, The Rocking Chair Reader—Family Gatherings* by Adams Media, *To Have and To Hold: Prayers, Poems, and Blessings for Newlyweds* by Time Warner's Centre Street Books, and *Pocket Prayers* by Chronicle Books. She is the author of a new poetry collection, *Prisms In A Looking Glass,* available from Lulu.com.

Mary Cook is a UK-based freelance writer and former newspaper reporter. Her poems, articles, and short stories have appeared in numerous publications, both in print and online. She has worked as an overseas correspondent for the Tokyo-based *Hiragana Times* and is the author of two self-help e-books at www.toptipsto.com. The most important aspect of her life is her Nichiren Shoshu Buddhist faith, which means she avoids Christmas celebrations as far as possible.

Laurie Corzett (libramoon) publishes the visionary art e-zine *Emerging Visions* (see emergingvisions.blogspot.com). You can also see more of her work on her Blog, *libramoon's observatory,* at www.lulu.com/libramoon and her website at www.geocities.com/ libramoon.geo/.

Kevin Craig has had poetry published in *Regina Weese, Quills Canadian Poetry Magazine, Jones Av. Journal, Heritage Writer, The Future Looks Bright Anthology,* and *Poetry Canada,* to name a few. His articles have been published in *The Globe & Mail, The Toronto Sun, Esteem Magazine, Word Weaver,* and *Oshawa This Week.* He has recorded spoken word memoir for CBC Radio Canada. His website is www.thewritelines.ca.

Freelance writer **Christine Cristiano** hangs her hat in Ontario, Canada. Her work has appeared in numerous print and online venues throughout Canada and the U.S. She is also the author of *Obsessed: Diary of a Freelance Writer.*

Richard Crowhurst is a freelance writer from Lincolnshire, England. He writes about many things but specializes in British history and heritage subjects. He is a keen amateur genealogist and (with help) has researched his own family history back to the early 1600s.

Ruth Dickson is the author of seven books, including the notorious *Married Men Make the Best Lovers.* Her nomadic lifestyle has taken her around the world, working in a wide variety of fields, including advertising, radio and television copywriting, teaching, and life coaching. After a thirty-year retirement, she resumed writing on her eightieth birthday, when she discovered blogging. These days, she airs her controversial views under the screen name "Supercrone" on Gather.com. Her witty, acerbic observations on sex, politics, religion, and achieving Crone status have made her one of the most popular contributors to this site, as well as to Blogster.com where she writes under the name "Octogenarian".

Betty Dobson is an award-winning creative writer whose work has appeared in *Apollo's Lyre, Brady Magazine, Eros & Rust, Jerry Jazz Musician, Sol Magazine,* and *Toasted Cheese,* as well as in several anthologies and through the Amazon Shorts program. She released her first poetry collection, *Paper Wings,* in 2006 and is hard at work on her first short fiction collection. She is also the owner of InkSpotter Publishing, a partner in Done East Productions, the Editor of *Poetry Canada* magazine, the Networking Editor with *WE Magazine for Women,* and the Contributing Poetry Editor with *Apollo's Lyre.* Her personal website is www.bettydobson.ca.

Krys Douglas teaches Humanities, Religion, Theatre, and Cultural Studies at Central New Mexico Community College. She won a fifth grade prize for a poem she wrote and has been writing ever since. She has published numerous academic articles and several short stories and poems. She is currently at work on a novel about medieval Iceland.

E.D. Easley has been writing and editing fiction too long. After four clinical deaths, he still doesn't know The Secrets of The Universe and flunked elementary algebra. The worst lies about him are at edeasley.blogspot.com.

Diana M. Hartman is a writer, mother of three, and a U.S. Marine spouse currently residing in Stuttgart, Germany.

Gary R. Hoffman taught English and Speech/Drama for twenty-two years in Missouri and California. He quit teaching over twenty years ago to go into business for himself. He now lives in a motor home and says, "Home is where you park it!" He travels the North American Continent, with Sandy and their cat Callie, and attempts to stay in moderate climates. He has had many short stories published in anthologies, e-zines, and magazines. He has also won many awards for his short stories.

Carolyn Howard-Johnson is an instructor for UCLA's Writers' Program and the author of two award-winning books, *This is the Place* and *Harkening*. Her how-to book for writers, *The Frugal Book Promoter: How to Do What Your Publisher Won't*, is the winner of *USA Book News*' Best Professional Book of 2004 and the Irwin Award. Her newsletter *Sharing with Writers* recently earned a Virtual Quill award from Bev Walton-Porter, editor/publisher of *Scribe & Quill*. Her most recent books are *Tracings*, a poetry chapbook, and *The Frugal Editor*, a follow-up to her successful *Frugal Book Promoter*.

Linda J. Hutchinson is a freelance writer and copywriter living in central Ohio. She has written for magazines, trade journals, newspapers, newsletters, websites, and e-zines. As at home on a construction site as in an art gallery, she's been told she "cleans up real good". She's currently at work on a non-fiction book and a novel, and has been writing a lot of humour lately. Learn more by visiting her website at www.lindajhutchinson.com.

Kristin Johnson is co-author of the "highly recommended" Midwest Book Review pick, *Christmas Cookies Are For Giving: Stories, Recipes and Tips for Making Heartwarming Gifts*. A downloadable media kit is available at www.christmascookiesareforgiving.com, or e-mail the publisher at info@tyrpublishing.com to receive a printed media kit and sample copy of the book. More articles are available at www.bakingchristmascookies.com.

Sheryl Kurland, writer, speaker, and author of *Everlasting Matrimony: Pearls Of Wisdom From Couples Married 50 Years Or More*, interviewed seventy-five couples across the U.S. to reveal the "real-life" secrets to lasting, loving relationships. Visit her website at www.EverlastingMatrimony.com.

Andrea MacEachern is a freelance writer currently living in St. John's, Newfoundland. She is also employed as a customer service agent in a local call centre and volunteers her spare time as a cameraperson with Roger's television for local talk show *Out of the Fog*. She has diplomas in Media Communications, Video Production, and Business. In the year 2000, she had the opportunity to participate in the Nova Scotia First Works Program in which she took on the role of co-writing the script for a thirty-minute video titled *Same Thing Different Day* and is currently working on her own feature length movie script.

Mary McIntosh, now eighty-six years old, is busily writing her memoir based on a five-year diary she kept as a teenager (and still has) from 1935-1939. Her goal is to see it published before she turns ninety. She has been published in *Lifeboat* (Autumn 2002), *Stops Along the Way*, *Good Old Days* magazine, *Bylines 2006 Writer's Desk Calendar*, and various online publications. Mary now lives in St. Petersburg, Florida, and attends a large writing/critiquing group each Saturday, of which she is the Secretary. Her non-writing activities include reading and swimming.

Writing is one of **Mamta Murthy**'s primary passions. Her works of fiction and feature articles have appeared in several leading national (India) and international publications. Besides technology trends and writing, she is also passionate about photography and travel.

Michelle V. Pozar, a fifty-two-year-old former substance abuse counsellor, grew up in a mill town, at the base of the Cascade Mountains, in Oregon's South Willamette Valley. Between her love of human nature and its expression, she continuously seeks to delve deeper into life's anomalies. She has been a featured op-editor in Seattle area papers and recently had a flash fiction piece published in *The Rose and Thorn Literary Magazine*.

Thelly Reahm is seventy-seven years young. She is Dick's wife, Bruce and Kat's mom, Gramma to six, Great-Gramma to twelve. She loves Life Story Writing, Seaside Presbyterian Church, going on cruises, crocheting baby clothes for Birth Choice, photography, and drop-in friends at Cardiff by the Sea, California. She believes it's important to leave our faith and values, family traditions, and just plain funny happenings about our family to the next generation. She's written over 500 stories about her family in her memoir *Tidbits of Time* and encourages many others to do the same at Life Story Writing. (For more information on Life Story Writing, see www.lifestorywriting.net and groups.yahoo.com/group/life-story-writing.)

Jacqueline Seewald has taught writing courses including Creative Writing at the high school, middle school, and college level and has also worked as an academic librarian and educational media specialist. Six of her novels have previously been published. A new novel, *The Inferno Collection*, was released by Five Star/Thomson/Gale (June 2007). Her poems, short stories, essays, reviews, and articles have appeared in numerous publications, such as *Sasee, Affaire de Coeur, Lost Treasure, Romance Rag, The Christian Science Monitor, Pedestal, Surreal, After Dark, The Dana Literary Society Journal, Palace of Reason, Library Journal,* and *Publishers Weekly.* She was twice a winner in the Writer's Digest Creative Writing Contest for poetry.

Susan Stephenson is a freelance writer based on the Australian east coast. She specializes in copyediting, children's writing, and travel writing. You may read about Susan's published work at www.coffscoastwriters.com/about.html.

Malcolm Watts is a writer, photographer, and soon-to-be-retired mental health professional. His interests range from fiction to photojournalism, history, parapsychology, and quantum Science. Read inside Malcolm's coming of age novel of the Sixties, *Reflections from Shadow*, at Amazon.com. His writing site and world travel photography gallery may be viewed online at www.authorsden.com/malcolmwatts.

Author Index

Barnes, Roy A.
  December 56

Beach-Jacobson, Roberta
  Turkey Therapy 41

Bryant, Gilda V.
  The Christmas Dragon 73

Burden, George
  Days of the Dead 25

Caplan, Janet
  Hanukah Harry 97

Close Mills, Michelle
  Flags 33

Cook, Mary
  Christmas Grows on Trees 61
  Cut-Price Paradise 19
  Joyful Noise 93

Corzett, Laurie
  Christmas trees enthralled in light 76
  Easter 16
  Holiday Giving 52
  Hurrah the Saturnalia 86
  Winter Solstice 66

Craig, Kevin
  Christmas in Miramichi 84
  So This is Christmas 50

Cristiano, Christine
  Thirteen Plates 71

Crowhurst, Richard
  Deck the Halls… 69

Dickson, Ruth
   Oy! It's Christmas Again! 68

Dobson, Betty
   A Bunch of Rocks: The Environmental Gutting of Malta 21
   Always Home 49
   Boxing Day at the North Pole 90
   Their Names Liveth Forevermore 31
   Unresolved 4

Douglas, Krys
   Luminarias 85

Easley, E.D.
   How Easter Really Began 9
   The Day After Thanksgiving Holiday 43

Hartman, Diana M.
   Christmas Alight 81
   Happy Holidays You Bah-Hum-Buggin' Vamps 67

Hoffman, Gary
   Our Little Floozy 79

Howard-Johnson, Carolyn
   Musing Over a New Calendar 3
   New Year 6

Hutchinson, Linda J.
   Excess and Dad's Exes 42

Johnson, Kristin
   A Dash of Cinnamon, a Pinch of the Past, a Smidgen of the Future 77

Kurland, Sheryl
   Peace On Earth…and In Your Home, Too 91

MacEachern, Andrea
   A Time Honoured Tradition 53

McIntosh, Mary
   Dear Santa 57

Murthy, Mamta
    Tracing Back Thanksgiving Tradition..37

Pozar, Michelle V.
    Christmas Without You 63

Reahm, Thelly
    Black-Eyed Peas and Ham Hocks 5
    The First Thanksgiving...39

Seewald, Jacqueline
    Miracle 99

Stephenson, Susan
    Australian Christmas Holiday..59

Watts, Malcolm
    Reflections from Shadow 87